STUDY GUIDE

MAMA BEAR

Apologetics

HILLARY MORGAN FERRER

HARVEST HOUSE PUBLISHERS
EUGENE, OREGON

All Scripture quotations are taken from The ESV® Bible (The Holy Bible, English Standard Version®), copyright © 2001 by Crossway, a publishing ministry of Good News Publishers. Used by permission. All rights reserved.

Cover design by Harvest House Publishers and Faceout Studio

Cover photo © CSA-Archive / Getty Images

MAMA BEAR APOLOGETICS is a registered trademark of Hillary Morgan Ferrer. Harvest House Publishers, Inc., is the exclusive licensee of the trademark MAMA BEAR APOLOGETICS.

For bulk, special sales, or ministry purchases, please call 1-800-547-8979. Email: Customerservice@hhpbooks.com

Mama Bear Apologetics® Study Guide
Copyright © 2021 by Hillary Morgan Ferrer
Published by Harvest House Publishers
Eugene, Oregon 97408
www.harvesthousepublishers.com

ISBN 978-0-7369-8379-2 (pbk)
ISBN 978-0-7369-8380-8 (eBook)

All rights reserved. No part of this publication may be reproduced, stored in a retrieval system, or transmitted in any form or by any means—electronic, mechanical, digital, photocopy, recording, or any other—except for brief quotations in printed reviews, without the prior permission of the publisher.

Printed in the United States of America

21 22 23 24 25 26 27 28 / BP-RD / 10 9 8 7 6

This book is dedicated to all the Mama Bears (and Papa Bears) who have answered the call to empower their kids to fearlessly interact with culture in love.

And to my lifetime ministry partner, John Ferrer. You are the sloth to my squirrel! Mama Bear would be impossible without you. You have paved the way, my love.

Also to my beating hearts,

Luke,

Joey,

Carmen,

and Ethan.

Acknowledgments

This study guide was a total labor of love, and I am so thankful that my Mama Bears are always available to lend support and advice! For Teasi Cannon, who took my pile of questions and made a more cohesive flow out of the chaos. (Y'all can all thank Teasi for the active reading chart at the beginning of each chapter.) For Amanda Burke, for being willing to talk through practical ideas for the moms. For our amazing Mama Bears who answered the call at the last hour to give me feedback with a two-day turnaround: Paige Jackson, Beth Barber, Kim Huxley, Karen Patrick, Janet Winn, Rebecca Dikeman, Hillary Short—y'all are rock stars.

CONTENTS

Welcome, and How to Use this Study Guide 7

Part 1: Rise Up, Mama Bears

1. Calling All Mama Bears: *My kid has a cheerio up
   his nose. Why am I reading this book?* 15

2. How to Be a Mama Bear: *Is this code for being the
   weirdest mom on the playground?* 21

3. The Discerning Mama Bear: *The refined art of
   "chew and spit"* 29

4. Linguistic Theft: *Redefining words to get your way
   and avoid reality* 37

**Part 2: Lies You've Probably Heard but Didn't Know
What They Were Called**

5. God Helps Those Who Help
   Themselves—*Self-Helpism*...................... 47

6. My Brain Is Trustworthy...According to
   My Brain—*Naturalism*........................ 57

7. I'd Believe in God if There Were Any Shred
   of Evidence—*Skepticism*....................... 69

8. The Truth Is, There Is
   No Truth—*Postmodernism* 79

9. You're Wrong to Tell Me that
   I'm Wrong!—*Moral Relativism* 91

10. Follow Your Heart—It Never
    Lies!—*Emotionalism* 103

11. Just Worship Something—*Pluralism*. 115

12. I'm Not Religious;
    I'm Spiritual!—*New Spirituality* 125

13. Communism Failed Because Nobody
    Did It Right—*Marxism* 137

14. The Future Is Female—*Feminism* 149

15. Christianity Needs
    a Makeover—*Progressive Christianity* 161

WELCOME, AND
HOW TO USE
THIS STUDY GUIDE

Welcome! We are thrilled you've chosen to use this study guide. Our sincere desire is that as you work through this guide, you will be gently challenged but not at all overwhelmed. With that in mind, we want to share some tips on how to make the most of your reading and this guide.

Before you read a chapter in the *Mama Bear Apologetics* book:

- We would love for you to have a four-color retractable click pen (flashback to high school!) on hand, but if you don't, grab four different colored pencils, pens, or highlighters and use a system similar to the one we are recommending below in **While you read**.

- Have a dictionary or dictionary app ready for reference.

- Pray and ask the Holy Spirit to guide you into all truth.

- Skim through the chapter title and bold-print subheads to get an idea of what you're going to read (this is a pre-reading strategy that helps get you excited to dig in).

- Think of a question or two you hope will be answered in the chapter.

While you read the chapter:

I have used this multicolor note-taking system for almost a decade. It has helped me to actively read and organize material so that, even years later, I can go back and glance through the book for the main points and my favorite quotes. The strategy suggested here is a simplified version of my system, so you can tweak it for what works best for you. I find that color-coding is helpful for future reference purposes:

- Black ink—draw a box around unfamiliar words and draw a squiggly line under the definition *if* it appears within the text. (Squiggly lines will help you distinguish definitions from general notes.) If the word is not defined, record definitions in the margins or at the back of the book. We recommend looking up the word meanings right away!

- Blue ink—underline generally helpful passages for easy skimming. This will help you when you search through the book later for the main ideas.

- Green ink—use this color for content that you have questions about. (I also draw a question mark in the margin.)

- Red ink or highlight—save this for the true "Aha!" moments or ideas you want to remember. (This is especially helpful for finding key quotes and thoughts in the future.)

After you read the chapter:

- Quickly skim through the chapter to review all the words you've underlined, highlighted, and written in the margins. (Look at all those colors—this is your pat on the back for being an active reader!)

- Jump into the study guide material for that chapter.

In each chapter of the study guide you will find an introductory thought followed by six major sections. We want you to set your own pace, so we haven't divided the lessons or sections into specific days, but you could choose to work through one section a day Monday through Friday. Here are the sections:

Active Reading Notes: Here you will record a few pre-, mid-, and post-reading thoughts, including vocabulary (see example and fuller explanation below).

Active Reading Notes (sample and explanations)

READING FOCUS:	MY RESPONSE:
Before you read:	
After skimming the chapter title and subheads, what is one question you would like to have answered in the chapter?	My question: Does protecting my kids mean sheltering them?
While you read:	
Vocabulary: Here you will list three words *you* found in the chapter, and we will add a few words we want to make sure you find.	My words: Here, write down words that are unfamiliar to you, and make your best attempt to briefly record the definition. Book words: Here, you'll find words that are defined in the book. Page numbers are given so that you can fill in the definitions in this space.
After you read:	
Answer: Did you find an answer to your pre-reading question? (We hope so.) If yes, write it here.	My answer: Protecting will involve some sheltering, but the best protection is teaching them how to discern for themselves.
"Aha!" Moments: List three things you highlighted or underlined in the chapter. This can be new information you learned or encouraging reinforcements of things you knew. Or just plain anything that popped out at you.	My "Aha!" moments: 1. 2. 3.

Empowering Words: Supplemental and significant vocabulary will be given here.

Empowering Thoughts: Supplemental or reinforcing thoughts will be included here.

Digging Deeper: Here we will ask some guiding questions to help you process what you've learned and further equip you to Roar Like a Mother. But be aware! Not all the questions are simple "regurgitate what the book said" kinds of questions. Many are intended to make you *think* through the material, drawing connections and wrestling through real-life scenarios. But don't worry! If you get stuck on a question, just move on until you feel more comfortable digging in. Or better yet, grab some girlfriends for coffee and discuss it! Whether or not you answer every single question, you *will* come away from this study guide with a much deeper grasp of what you're learning.

Key Scriptures: Here we've offered a few related scriptures that can help you reflect on what God says regarding some of the ideas presented in each chapter. We recommend journaling through each of them, evaluating *how* the passages reinforce or address the biblical perspective of the topic at hand.

Paws for Prayer: Here you will be guided in a sweet time of prayer—a time to take what you're learning to God and to intentionally involve the Holy Spirit in your journey. The PAWS for prayer section has four steps:

PRAISE—Identify the *attributes* of God that you have seen manifested lately. You may be thankful *for* a recent bonus, but you will want to *praise* God for being Jehovah Rapha, the God who provides. Or, maybe you didn't get the bonus and you don't know why. *Praise* God for His omniscience and how He knows what you need when you need it, even if you don't understand. Praising God for *who* He is rather than *what* He does will help you orient your heart toward Him, no matter what is going on in your life, good or bad. If you need a little help with this section, I recommend googling "attributes of God" or "names of God."

ADMIT—Acknowledge the areas where you have blown it. Maybe you didn't trust God, or you acted in anger with your kids or husband. Whatever your dirty laundry, bring it to God here. He already knows your heart and wants to be with you as you learn to navigate this thing called the Christian life.

WORSHIP through thanksgiving—Here is where you can thank God for specific things He has *done*. When you remember that all good things come from Him, you realize you have much to be thankful for.

SUPPLICATION (or SUBMIT your requests)—After you have praised God for who He is, admitted where you are struggling, and worshipped through thanksgiving, then present your requests to Him. Sometimes God doesn't give us what we ask for because we ask with wrong motives (James 4:3). Or sometimes what we want would thwart something that He—in His goodness and knowledge—is doing in our lives that couldn't be accomplished if He answered our specific wish. But He still wants us to ask, and we can know that however He chooses to answer, it is for our good. How awesome is that?

Part 1

RISE UP, MAMA BEARS

In Part 1, we learn what it means to be a Mama (or Papa) Bear and why our desire to empower our kids is so important and timely! We learn about the youth exodus—what it is, and why we should be concerned. We also gain clarity on what real discernment is while exposing one of the enemy's most confusing tactics: *linguistic theft*.

We hope the following pages will shed light on the cultural confusion you're likely experiencing on a daily basis *and* empower you to have God-honoring conversations with your friends, neighbors, and children. We want you to have tools that will help you think critically about the issues of our day. Critical thinking doesn't mean you are *criticizing* anything. Rather, it means that you are able to analyze information, evaluate its sources and content, and make reasonable judgments as to the pros and cons of the idea. This will give you the confidence to dignify secular worldviews while respectfully demonstrating how a biblical approach best addresses common concerns.

Are you ready to chew and spit and Roar Like a Mother? Let's go, Mama Bears!

LESSON 1

CALLING ALL
MAMA BEARS

As parents—as well as aunts, uncles, grandparents, and guardians—one of our most important jobs is preparing kids for the real world. Our children are growing up in a society that is vastly different than the one in which we grew up. I loved memorizing Bible verses as a child, but I didn't have to deal with the culture telling me that the Bible was full of contradictions or that it was just a book of fairy tales. The trustworthiness of Scripture was presumed. That is not the case anymore. We can no longer rely on Western culture to reinforce our Christian beliefs, and we cannot ignore the fact that youth are leaving the church in droves. What many parents don't know is that some of the reasons for their departure are totally preventable.

Mama Bear Apologetics, page 22

ACTIVE READING NOTES

READING FOCUS:	MY RESPONSE:
Before you read:	
After skimming the chapter title and subheads, what is one question you would like to have answered in the chapter?	My question:

While you read:	
Vocabulary: Here you will list three words *you* found in the chapter and a few words we want to make sure you found.	My words: Book words: *Youth exodus* (page 27)—

After you read:	
Answer: Did you find an answer to your pre-reading question? (We hope so.) If yes, record it to the right.	My answer:
"Aha!" Moments: List three things you high-lighted or underlined in the chapter. This can be new information you learned or encouraging reinforcements of things you knew. Or just plain anything that popped out at you.	My "Aha!" moments: 1. 2. 3.

EMPOWERING WORDS

- *Apologetics*—From the Greek term *apologia* ("answer/ defense"). Means to give a reasoned answer for why one believes something to be true.

- *Agnosticism*—Belief that one doesn't know or cannot know whether God exists. People who hold this view are called agnostics.

- *Moralistic therapeutic deism*—A general belief that God exists, but only to make you a happier, better (but not necessarily *holier*) person. The term is from Christian

Smith and Melinda Denton, *Soul Searching and Spiritual Lives of American Teenagers* (2005).

- *Generation X*—People born between (roughly) 1965–1979.
- *Generation Z*—People born between (roughly) 1995–2010, mostly children of Gen Xers. This generation is also known as "digital natives" because they grew up with the Internet and smart phones. This group trends politically liberal and religiously "none" (no formal religious affiliation). Their interactions on social media play a huge role in their sense of self.
- *Skepticism*—A method, habit, or tendency to doubt. People who identify themselves as skeptics are usually referring to religious skepticism.

EMPOWERING THOUGHTS

When it comes to teaching children the difference between right and wrong thinking, there are basically three approaches parents use:

- Reactionary—you take action *after* a problem has arisen
- Responsive—you take action *while* the problem is taking place
- Anticipatory—you take action *before* the problem arises

Why do you think so many parents tend to default toward the reactionary approach?

While there is extra work involved in using the anticipatory approach, what are some advantages of taking this path?

Sometimes all we can do is take the reactionary approach (I mean, we can't foresee *all* possible problems before they arise). However, which of these approaches is best suited for children's spiritual growth?

DIGGING DEEPER

Why Apologetics Is So Important for Parents

1. How do *both* emotions and knowledge (i.e., head *and* heart) build a house of faith? Do you have a tendency to rely more heavily on one or the other (pages 23-26)? Why do you think that is?

2. Read the story of the Ferrers' pastor (pages 25-26). How did the pastor feel *before* he went to John's debate? How did he feel after? What changed his mind?

3. What did you think about apologetics before you read this chapter? Has your view changed after reading, and if so, how?

The Youth Exodus

4. In what ways have you personally experienced the youth exodus—
either in your generation while growing up or in your children's
generation?

5. Were the results of the Barna Survey listed on page 29 shocking to
you? Which two statistics do you find to be the most troubling? Do
you feel equipped to navigate doubts and struggles like this? (If not,
no worries. You're in the right place!)

KEY SCRIPTURES

We encourage you to read the following verses in context (read at
least the entire chapter), reflect on how they relate to what you're learning, and thank God for the hope and guidance found in His Word.

- *Colossians 2:8*—"See to it that no one takes you captive by
  philosophy and empty deceit, according to human tradition, according to the elemental spirits of the world, and
  not according to Christ."

- *1 Timothy 6:20-21*—"Guard the deposit entrusted to you.
  Avoid the irreverent babble and contradictions of what is
  falsely called 'knowledge,' for by professing it some have
  swerved from the faith."

- *Proverbs 22:6*—"Train up a child in the way he should go;
  even when he is old he will not depart from it."

PAWS FOR PRAYER

In closing this chapter, reflect on what you learned in Lesson 1 and journal your prayer to God here.

Praise:

Admit:

Worship with thanksgiving:

Supplication (ask):

HOW TO BE
A MAMA BEAR

Moms do what it takes, no matter how hard, and no matter how gross. While this kind of dedication is important for our children's physical development, it is especially imperative when it comes to our children's *spiritual development*. We may not *want* to jump into the deep end of theology and apologetics, but we *will*, lest we see our kids dragged down by the rushing rapids of bad ideas. We're Mama Bears. That's what we do! A Mama Bear does whatever it takes, even if that means studying apologetics.

Mama Bear Apologetics, page 36

ACTIVE READING NOTES

READING FOCUS:	MY RESPONSE:
Before you read:	
After skimming the chapter title and subheads, what is one question you would like to have answered in the chapter?	My question:

While you read:	
Vocabulary: Here you will list three words *you* found in the chapter and a few words we want to make sure you found.	My words: Book words: *Apologetics* (page 37)— *Reason* (pages 37-38)—
After you read:	
Answer: Did you find an answer to your pre-reading question? (We hope so.) If yes, record it to the right.	My answer:
"Aha!" Moments: List three things you high-lighted or underlined in the chapter. This can be new information you learned or encouraging reinforcements of things you knew. Or just plain anything that popped out at you.	My "Aha!" moments: 1. 2. 3.

EMPOWERING WORDS

- *Truth*—That which corresponds to reality (regardless of our feelings about the situation).

- *Finite*—Having boundaries or limits.

- *Infinite*—Not having boundaries or limits.

- *Evidence*—Data on which to base proofs or to support establishing what is true or false; the physical or philosophical grounds or basis for belief or disbelief.

EMPOWERING THOUGHTS

We would like to take this moment to give you some extra encouragement. We know that Mama Bears are in all sorts of different stages of motherhood. Some of us have older children and can easily carve out lengthy study times. Others are homeschooling or have toddlers clinging to them—even in the bathroom.

With that in mind, we want to encourage you to keep your eyes on Jesus and your own *why* and *who*. Why are you reading this book? Why do you want to learn more? Who do you want to encourage and empower?

We also want to encourage you *not* to compare yourself with other Mama Bears. Comparison kills. We must offer Jesus what we individually can give of ourselves, and that includes the amount of mental energy we have.

Before you continue this worthy journey of loving God (and your kids) with your mind, take a moment to record your *why* and *who* in the spaces below. Keep that and Jesus in mind every step of the way.

My *why*—

My *who*—

DIGGING DEEPER

1. Read the section "What a Mama Bear Is (and Isn't)" (pages 39-40). How has the Lord been preparing you to be a Mama Bear?

2. Read "Four Key Traits of Mama Bears" (pages 40-42). What are the four *H*s of Mama Bears? Briefly describe the importance of each trait:

H ....

H ....

H ....

H ....

3. Review "I'm New to Apologetics. Where Do I Even Start?" (pages 42-44), then answer the questions in the boxes below.

Know Your Bible

Why is this important?	How can I implement this?

Gather Resources

Why is this important?	How can I implement this?

Carve Out Regular Family Time to Study

Why is this important?	How can I implement this?

Find Like-Minded Mamas

Why is this important?	How can I implement this?

Practice, Practice, Practice

Why is this important?	How can I implement this?

4. Which of the above points would be the easiest for you to implement, and which is most outside your comfort zone? Why?

KEY SCRIPTURES

We encourage you to read the following verses in context (read at least the entire chapter), reflect on how they relate to what you're learning, and thank God for the hope and guidance found in His Word.

- *2 Corinthians 10:5*—"We destroy arguments and every lofty opinion raised against the knowledge of God, and take every thought captive to obey Christ."

- *1 Peter 3:15*—"In your hearts honor Christ the Lord as holy, always being prepared to make a defense to anyone who asks you for a reason for the hope that is in you; yet do it with gentleness and respect."

- *Jude 3*—"Although I was very eager to write to you about our common salvation, I found it necessary to write appealing to you to contend for the faith that was once for all delivered to the saints."

PAWS FOR PRAYER

In closing this chapter, reflect on what you learned in Lesson 2 and journal your prayer to God here.

Praise:

Admit:

Worship with thanksgiving:

Supplication (ask):

THE DISCERNING MAMA BEAR

Biblical discernment means identifying *both* the good and the bad. I compare biblical discernment to having a food allergy. For example, I can't eat peas. (Or rather, I *can*, but it is an unpleasant experience for everyone afterward.) If someone were to serve me a delicious plate of fried rice with vegetables, the first thing I would do is pick out the peas. I don't accept all the food, and I don't reject all of it. You could call this "culinary discernment." As Mama Bears, our job is to help separate the good from the bad, accept the good, and reject the bad.

Mama Bear Apologetics, page 48

ACTIVE READING NOTES

READING FOCUS:	MY RESPONSE:
Before you read:	
After skimming the chapter title and subheads, what is one question you would like to have answered in the chapter?	My question:

While you read:	
Vocabulary: Here you will list three words *you* found in the chapter and a few words we want to make sure you found.	My words: Book words: *Strawman argument* (page 56)— *Biblical wisdom/biblical worldview* (pages 58-59)—

After you read:	
Answer: Did you find an answer to your pre-reading question? (We hope so.) If yes, record it to the right.	My answer:
"Aha!" Moments: List three things you high-lighted or underlined in the chapter. This can be new information you learned or encouraging reinforcements of things you knew. Or just plain anything that popped out at you.	My "Aha!" moments: 1. 2. 3.

EMPOWERING WORDS

- *Argue*—To provide reasons or evidence that supports an idea or belief in a persuasive way.

- *Culture*—Generally refers to the customs, ways, practices, and behaviors of a people group or social group.

- *Discernment*—Having keen insight with accurate and true judgment.

EMPOWERING THOUGHTS

We really, really want to make sure you understand how to ROAR like a Mama Bear! Using the ROAR method, as described on pages 53-60 in the book *Mama Bear Apologetics*, is one of the most important aspects of being a Mama Bear. For reinforcement, carefully answer the following questions:

The Book's Definition	In Your Own Words
R—	
O—	
A—	
R—	

Why is it important to identify both the good and the bad in cultural messages (pages 54 and 57)?

Based on what you've learned, how can the ROAR method help generate respectful and productive conversation?

DIGGING DEEPER

1. Christianity can have the reputation of being "the party of no" (page 48). How might Christians have gained that reputation? What could we do instead?

2. Explain the all-safe/dangerous approach to discernment (pages 49-50). Can you give examples of times when you have been guilty of using this method?

3. What are some negative consequences our kids might experience when we use the all-safe/dangerous method (pages 52-53)?

4. In three or four sentences, describe the chew-and-spit method of discernment, and how it differs from the all-safe/dangerous method (pages 50-51).

5. Below are listed three key steps toward exercising discernment (pages 56-58). In your own words, list the importance of each step.

Step Toward Discernment	Why this Step Is Important
Seeing things accurately	
Correctly identifying the good	
Correctly identifying the bad	

6. The band AC/DC was created in the 1970s. The idea for the band's name came up when one of the band members noticed the AC/DC label on an electrical appliance. Some people started denouncing the band, claiming that the name meant "anti-Christ/devil's children." Which step(s) of discernment do you think went missing when those claims were made?

KEY SCRIPTURES

We encourage you to read the following verses in context (read at least the entire chapter), reflect on how they relate to what you're learning, and thank God for the hope and guidance found in His Word.

- *Philippians 1:9-10*—"It is my prayer that your love may abound more and more, with knowledge and all discernment, so that you may approve what is excellent, and so be pure and blameless for the day of Christ."

- *Colossians 4:6*—"Let your speech always be gracious, seasoned with salt, so that you may know how you ought to answer each person."

- *Hebrews 5:14*—"Solid food is for the mature, for those who have their powers of discernment trained by constant practice to distinguish good from evil."

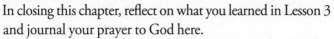

PAWS FOR PRAYER

In closing this chapter, reflect on what you learned in Lesson 3 and journal your prayer to God here.

Praise:

Admit:

Worship with thanksgiving:

Supplication (ask):

LINGUISTIC THEFT

Linguistic theft is much more sinister than just the evolution of language. *Linguistic theft refers to purposefully hijacking words, changing their definitions, and then using those same words as tools of propaganda.* This is not a new technique (it's an especially virulent form of the equivocation fallacy), but it is extremely prevalent right now. Not only are words in general being commandeered to promote the lies we discuss in this book, but *Christian* words, virtues, and concepts are being kidnapped as well. And the ransom—acquiescence to the new definition—is too high a price to pay.

Mama Bear Apologetics, page 63

ACTIVE READING NOTES

READING FOCUS:	MY RESPONSE:
Before you read:	
After skimming the chapter title and subheads, what is one question you would like to have answered in the chapter?	My question:

While you read:	
Vocabulary: Here you will list three words *you* found in the chapter and a few words we want to make sure you found.	My words: Book words: *Linguistic theft* (page 63)— *Amygdala* (page 66)—The site of the brain involved with _____ processing. *Prefrontal cortex* (page 66)—The site of the brain involved with _____ _____.
After you read:	
Answer: Did you find an answer to your pre-reading question? (We hope so.) If yes, record it to the right.	My answer:
"Aha!" Moments: List three things you highlighted or underlined in the chapter. This can be new information you learned or encouraging reinforcements of things you knew. Or just plain anything that popped out at you.	My "Aha!" moments: 1. 2. 3.

EMPOWERING WORDS

- *Innate*—An internal tendency, something that is inborn or natural.
- *Fight-or-flight response*—A physical (and hormonal)

response to a stressful situation (either physically or emotionally) that triggers a rush of adrenaline so that one can either run away or fight. In this state, people often act on instinct and not reason. Modern definitions include the freeze response, where a person freezes and is unable to respond to the situation.

- *Rational*—Based on reason, sound judgment, logic, or common sense.

- *Propaganda*—Information that advocates a position using only favorable evidence, sometimes even twisting the situation so that the desired ideology always sounds like the right course of action.

- *Social construct*—An idea that is not based in ultimate reality but has been created and upheld by members of a society (and thus can be changed at will based on popular opinion).

- *Argue*—To provide reasons or evidence that supports an idea or belief in a persuasive way.

EMPOWERING THOUGHTS

This chapter is a meaty one! So get your Bible handy, because you will be doing a lot of Scripture work for this lesson.

The English language is flexible and changes. New words are invented. Old words drop out of usage. Still other words take on new meaning and significance. Sometimes it's a matter of fashion trends, other times it's an aimless accident of modern culture. Language can change over time. How is normal change different from linguistic theft?

John 1:1 says, "In the beginning was the Word [Greek, *logos*], and the Word [*logos*] was with God, and the Word [*logos*] was God." What does Christ as "the Word" tell us about the importance of words?

The name *Satan* means "adversary." An adversary is someone (a person or group) or something (an ideology) that opposes or attacks relentlessly. Isn't that exactly what Satan is doing against the things of God? Below is a list of the five tactics utilized by those who commit linguistic theft. In what ways do these tactics shut down fruitful and productive conversation (pages 65-68)?

- Stops a discussion in its tracks—

- Compels people to act without thinking through the issues—

- Blurs the details—

- Vilifies the opposing viewpoint—

- Turns a negative into a positive (or vice versa)—

DIGGING DEEPER

Take some time to read what the following verses say about the key words listed below. Some of these words won't be defined directly in a verse, but by looking up multiple verses and reading the surrounding context (several verses before and after), you can gain a good understanding of the biblical definition of these words. Feel free to use a concordance or Bible study app to look up more verses than those we've listed. Then describe what linguistic thieves typically mean when they use these same key words.

Biblical Understanding of Key Word	Secular Understanding of Key Word by Linguistic Thieves
Love (see 1 Corinthians 13:4-7; Philippians 1:9-11)—	*Love—*
Truth (see Psalm 119:160; John 8:31-32; John 17:17)—	*Truth—*
Tolerance (see Proverbs 17:15; Romans 12:18; Romans 14:1-4)—	*Tolerance—*
Justice (see Deuteronomy 27:19; Isaiah 1:17)—	*Justice—*

Equality (see Genesis 1:27; Romans 2:11; Galatians 3:28; James 2:8-9)—	*Equality*—
Bigot (see 1 Samuel 16:7; Acts 10:28; John 7:24; 1 John 2:11)—	*Bigot*—
Authentic (see John 3:19-21; James 2:18; 1 John 1:8-10; 1 John 3:18)—	*Authentic*—

KEY SCRIPTURES

We encourage you to read the following verses in context (read at least the entire chapter), reflect on how they relate to what you're learning, and thank God for the hope and guidance found in His Word.

- *Colossians 2:8*—"See to it that no one takes you captive by philosophy and empty deceit, according to human tradition, according to the elemental spirits of the world, and not according to Christ." (Hint: a person needs to use *words* to convey philosophy and to deceive someone.)

- *2 Peter 2:1-3*—"False prophets also arose among the people, just as there will be false teachers among you, who will secretly bring in destructive heresies, even denying the Master who bought them, bringing upon themselves swift destruction. And many will follow their sensuality, and because of them the way of truth will be blasphemed. And in their greed they will exploit you with false words." (Hint: Destructive heresies often use *words* and, especially

now, involve *the changing of historically understood* definitions of words. The difference between a heresy and an
orthodox statement might just be how the person is defin-
ing key words!)

- *Genesis 11:1-7*—"Now the whole earth had one language
  and the same words...Then they said, 'Come, let us build
  ourselves a city and a tower with its top in the heavens, and
  let us make a name for ourselves, lest we be dispersed over
  the face of the whole earth.' And the LORD came down
  to see the city and the tower, which the children of man
  had built. And the LORD said, 'Behold, they are one people, and they have all one language, and this is only the
  beginning of what they will do. And nothing [i.e., no evil
  thing] that they propose to do will now be impossible for
  them. Come, let us go down and there confuse their language, so that they may not understand one another's
  speech.'" (Hint: How important did God perceive a uni-
  versal understanding of words to be?)

- *Zephaniah 3:9*—"At that time I will change the speech
  of the peoples to a pure speech, that all of them may call
  upon the name of the LORD and serve him with one
  accord."

PAWS FOR PRAYER

In closing this chapter, reflect on what you learned in Lesson 4 and journal your prayer to God here.

Praise:

Admit:

Worship with thanksgiving:

Supplication (ask):

Part 2

LIES YOU'VE PROBABLY HEARD BUT DIDN'T KNOW WHAT THEY WERE CALLED

What is a worldview?

A worldview is the lens through which you perceive the world around you. It affects how you interpret your lived experience so that you draw certain conclusions about how the world works. It influences how you answer life's big questions: What does it mean to be human? Why are we here? Where did we come from? What is wrong with the world? How can it be fixed? Where are we headed? What is "the good life"—what do we mean by "good"?

For a worldview to be cohesive, the answers to these questions must not contradict one another. Most secular worldviews contradict themselves. For example, why would a worldview that claims our brains were formed by natural processes aimed at *survival* also claim that we should trust these brains to discern *ultimate truth*? Survival is not the same thing as truth. This worldview is not cohesive (and it's self-refuting to boot!). Or, what about the people who claim that the Christian sexual ethic is harmful, repressive, and archaic? They may casually sleep around and look down on Christians as prudes. Yet at the same time, they would feel monstrously betrayed if their significant other were to cheat on them. Their worldview is not cohesive. Sex either means something or it doesn't.

As Christians, we have a biblical worldview that is both cohesive and in line with reality—namely, the reality of humanity, which is broken by sin and the fall. The Christian worldview stands apart from the others in that—when properly understood—it can be applied to life's big questions, does not contradict itself, and results in a society that is orderly and safe. (Side note: *The Handmaid's Tale* is *not* built on a properly understood Christian worldview.)

Most people instinctively understand and agree that our world is broken, yet their diagnosis of our main problems (and thus solutions) can vary wildly. Any foundation that identifies something other than *sin* as the problem and *Christ* as the solution ultimately ends in idolatry—believing that something or someone other than God is the means for healing what is broken, or for bringing us happiness (that is, the good life).

GOD HELPS THOSE WHO HELP THEMSELVES—*SELF-HELPISM*

Self-helpism starts with a good idea—that we should do what we can, within our power, to work for a better life for ourselves and others. We can become better educated, set worthy goals and strive for them, discipline ourselves for positive ends, and encourage others to do the same. However, in the final analysis, we can't fix what is *fundamentally broken* within ourselves. Only God can do that. As the term *self-helpism* suggests, self-help is a completely unbiblical take on human brokenness. Its message (boiled way, way down) is that we need search no further than within ourselves to find both the causes and remedies for our brokenness...

To be fair, self-help isn't all bad. It's not like Scripture tells us to sit back and just pray about all our bad habits and watch them magically disappear. Rather, the message we would like to emphasize is that self-helpism has limits. There is a line between being good stewards of our bodies, emotions, and behaviors versus trying to change our own hearts or sin nature apart from the Holy Spirit's sanctifying work.

Mama Bear Apologetics, pages 82-83

ACTIVE READING NOTES

READING FOCUS:	MY RESPONSE:
Before you read:	
After skimming the chapter title and subheads, what is one question you would like to have answered in the chapter?	My question:
While you read:	
Vocabulary: Here you will list three words *you* found in the chapter and a few words we want to make sure you found.	My words: Book words: *Self-helpism* (page 82)—
After you read:	
Answer: Did you find an answer to your pre-reading question? (We hope so.) If yes, record it to the right.	My answer:
"Aha!" Moments: List three things you highlighted or underlined in the chapter. This can be new information you learned or encouraging reinforcements of things you knew. Or just plain anything that popped out at you.	My "Aha!" moments: 1. 2. 3.

EMPOWERING WORDS

- *Self-awareness*—Being aware of one's own good traits, bad traits, thoughts, motives, emotions, and behaviors.
- *Broken*—Not functioning as intended or designed.
- *Idolatry*—Excessive devotion or commitment to something or someone besides the one true God.
- *Deism*—The belief that God created the universe and ordered it according to natural and moral laws, but then left it on its own and does not intervene with what's happening.
- *Humanism*—Cultural and intellectual movement that affirms people's innate goodness, which is marred by their environment and upbringing. Humanism says that given the right tools, people can become good again by their own efforts.

EMPOWERING THOUGHTS

Purpose is the reason for which something or someone exists. One of the most amazing things about being a human is our primary or common purpose: We are God's image bearers (Genesis 1:26)! Another way to say this is that we are created to reflect or magnify God's character in the world.

Keeping our primary purpose in mind each day will help us to avoid the pitfalls of self-helpism. When we show a willingness to better ourselves—whether physically, emotionally, or intellectually—we reveal our desire to glorify God and love others to the best of our ability.

With our true purpose in mind, read the Norman Vincent Peale quote on page 86 of *Mama Bear Apologetics*.

Is there anything true in his statement? If so, what?

If taken at face value—without biblical correction—how might Peale's statement lead to an unhealthy striving?

Scripture can sometimes seem contradictory (but it never truly is). For example, in Psalm 46:10, the Lord says through David, "Be still, and know that I am God" (Psalm 46:10). Yet in 1 Timothy 4:9-11, we are called to "toil and strive" as we train in godliness (1 Timothy 4:9-11).

How can these both be true and godly ways to behave (hint: read Ecclesiastes 3:1-8)?

What are some examples of times that you need to "be still"? What are some examples of times that the Lord might be calling you to "toil and strive"?

DIGGING DEEPER

It's time to Roar Like a Mother at self-helpism!

Recognize the Message

1. With regard to self-helpism, define the following:

- the diagnosis (see pages 87-88)—

- the remedy (see page 88)—

- the source (see pages 88-89)—

Offer Discernment

2. Observe where self-helpism rightly identifies truths, as well as the lies that have snuck in with these truths:

	Truths identified	Lies that snuck in
Diagnosis		
Remedy		
Source		

Argue for a Healthier Approach

3. Choose one to three of the truths you identified above and interact with them. How does a balanced biblical approach achieve the goals

or affirm the truths that the proponents of self-helpism are offering? Bonus points for scripture references!

Reinforce Through Discussion, Discipleship, and Prayer

4. The apostle Paul was chosen by God and, after his conversion, dedicated his entire life to ministry and serving others. In contrast, self-helpism often teaches that Christianity is about living "your best life now." Read 2 Corinthians 11:23-29 together with your children.

What do you think Paul would have said in response to self-helpism's approach to living?

What do you think self-helpism would have told Paul to do differently and how would it have changed his ministry if he followed the advice?

5. The truth is, Christianity is not about our best lives now. Our best lives are yet to come, and the way we persevere in this life matters. The fact that Christians face difficulties and persecution in the midst of secular culture are not limited to the annals of history. It is happening now, in our lives, and it is important to familiarize our children with present-day persecuted Christians.

Voice of the Martyrs is an amazing organization that tracks persecution all over the world. Go to https://www.prisoneralert.com /vompw_prisoners.html and get to know some of the prisoners. Read their stories and discuss with your kids how many of today's Christian self-help books miss the point in light of the persecuted church.

You may want to go a step further and together, as a family, write letters of encouragement to the prisoners (go to https://www.pris oneralert.com/vompw_writing.htm). Choose a prisoner to encourage and write a letter with your children. *But first make sure to read over Prisoner Alert's guidelines!*

KEY SCRIPTURES

We encourage you to read the following verses in context (read at least the entire chapter), reflect on how they relate to what you're learning, and thank God for the hope and guidance found in His Word. (Hint: Each of these passages might be used to either *support* or *correct* self-helpism. You can also use them to determine what is within *God's* sphere of control versus what is reasonably within *our* sphere of control.)

- *Psalm 121:2*—"My help comes from the LORD, who made heaven and earth."

- *Ezekiel 36:26*—"I [God] will give you a new heart, and a new spirit I will put within you. And I will remove the heart of stone from your flesh and give you a heart of flesh."

- *Colossians 3:5-10*—"Put to death therefore what is earthly in you: sexual immorality, impurity, passion, evil desire, and covetousness, which is idolatry. On account of these the wrath of God is coming. In these you too once walked, when you were living in them. But now you must put them all away: anger, wrath, malice, slander, and obscene talk from your mouth. Do not lie to one another, seeing that you have put off the old self with its practices and have put on the new self, which is being renewed in knowledge after the image of its creator."

- *James 1:22*—"Be doers of the word, and not hearers only, deceiving yourselves."

PAWS FOR PRAYER

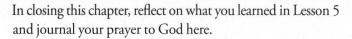

In closing this chapter, reflect on what you learned in Lesson 5 and journal your prayer to God here.

Praise:

Admit:

Worship with thanksgiving:

Supplication (ask):

MY BRAIN IS TRUSTWORTHY... ACCORDING TO MY BRAIN—*NATURALISM*

Naturalism is the belief that natural causes are sufficient to explain everything in our world, and *materialism* is the belief that nature (that is, material stuff) is all that exists. Material things can be studied with the five senses. Immaterial things (morals, the human soul, angels, demons, and God) cannot...However, the irony of claiming "The material world is all there is" is that this is a metaphysical—outside of the physical realm—or philosophical statement. The meaning of those words is not material. Not only is it immaterial and philosophical, but it is an *untestable assumption*, an allegation that is often brought against Christians...

There have been a whole schmear of hypotheses offered throughout history to explain away the existence of a God who is uncreated, self-existent, and powerful enough to create the universe. The solution? Hypothesize something *else* that is uncreated, self-existent, and capable of creating. Mama Bears, listen closely when I say this: Every hypothesis about origins is eventually reduced to something that (1) has always existed—is eternal, (2) needs no creator—is self-existent, and (3) is sufficiently powerful to create. Aristotle called this the "first cause." Do not let anyone tell you that their first cause is "more scientific" than yours.

Mama Bear Apologetics, pages 100, 105-106

ACTIVE READING NOTES

READING FOCUS:	MY RESPONSE:
Before you read:	
After skimming the chapter title and subheads, what is one question you would like to have answered in the chapter?	My question:
While you read:	
Vocabulary: Here you will list three words *you* found in the chapter and a few words we want to make sure you found.	My words: Book words: *Self-refuting statement* (page 99)— *Naturalism* (page 100)— *Materialism* (page 100)— *Faith* (pages 100-101)— *Supernatural* (page 101)—

After you read:	
Answer: Did you find an answer to your pre-reading question? (We hope so.) If yes, record it to the right.	My answer:
"Aha!" Moments: List three things you high-lighted or underlined in the chapter. This can be new information you learned or encouraging reinforcements of things you knew. Or just plain anything that popped out at you.	My "Aha!" moments: 1. 2. 3.

EMPOWERING WORDS

- *Believe*—Mental acceptance of ideas that one is convinced are true.

- *Knowledge*—Justified, true belief—not just a feeling that something is true, but reasoned and evidential conclusion that something is true, that in actuality is true (i.e., if there is no justification, or if it's not actually true, then it's not knowledge).

- *Scientific method*—The process of developing a conclusion through repeatable tests and experiments. Usually involves creating and testing a hypothesis in a way that can be repeated by others through the collection of data and forming a conclusion that confirms, rejects, or alters the original hypothesis.

- *Scientism*—The belief that science is the only trustworthy way for people to obtain knowledge.

EMPOWERING THOUGHTS

The Greek word translated "faith" is *pistis*, which includes an element of being *persuaded* (i.e., not blind faith).

What is usually required for you to become persuaded about something?

How is being persuaded different from conjuring up some feeling of belief?

Some respond to apologetics by saying, "If you knew everything, then you wouldn't need faith!" If evidence persuades you to be *more* assured and *more* convinced that Christianity is true, then what does that do for your faith, according to Hebrews 11:1? Increase it or decrease it?

One type of evidence that works very well to persuade is scientific data. But some of life's experiences and treasures cannot be measured or tested in a lab.

What are some things that exist but aren't suited to scientific testing?

Your child comes to you and asks, "How can we believe in God when we can't see Him and He can't be proven scientifically?" How do you respond (see pages 100-101)?

On pages 102-105 of *Mama Bear Apologetics,* we discuss the history of the four main philosophical periods: premodernism, modernism, postmodernism, and *whatever the heck we are in now* (basically a blend of the three periods, with a whole lot more emotionalism thrown in). These perspectives will be repeated in most other chapters, so getting a good grasp on them now is important.

A pivotal factor in each of these philosophical perspectives is how a person determines what is true—in other words, how do we *know* things? *Understanding how someone determines truth is imperative for understanding the best way to present the evidence for Christianity to them.* We want to meet people where they are.

Look at each of the following statements and circle which worldview they are coming from (some may have more than one answer). (Note: The answers are found on page 172.) If you are going through this workbook with a group, discuss how each of these premises would affect the way a person might be convinced of the truth of the gospel.

1. These people are more likely to treat a religious authority as their main source of truth.	Premod – Mod – Postmod
2. These people typically believe they can be certain about truth by reason alone and *not* by using their emotions or feelings.	Premod – Mod – Postmod
3. These people might abandon Christianity because one church service was boring, so it didn't "feel true" to them.	Premod – Mod – Postmod
4. It is *easy* for this person to trust Scripture, even if it doesn't make sense to them.	Premod – Mod – Postmod

5. These people are less likely to call something "true" unless there is a scientific study that backs it up.	Premod – Mod – Postmod
6. These people tend to put a higher emphasis on common sense as a source of truth.	Premod – Mod – Postmod
7. These people may treat testimonials or "before" and "after" pictures on a website as evidence of the effectiveness of a new medical procedure.	Premod – Mod – Postmod
8. These people place a heavy emphasis on personal experience as their source of truth.	Premod – Mod – Postmod
9. These people tend to treat scientists, celebrities, athletes, and talkative strangers as equal authorities—each having their own equally legitimate truth.	Premod – Mod – Postmod
10. These people tend to defer to tradition as the correct way to do something.	Premod – Mod – Postmod

DIGGING DEEPER

1. Fill in the blanks with help from pages 105-106 of *Mama Bear Apologetics*:

> Every hypothesis about origins [of the universe] is eventually reduced to something that (1) has always _____ — is _____, (2) needs no _____ —is _____, and (3) is sufficiently _____ to _____. Aristotle called this the "first cause." Don't let anyone tell you that their first cause is "more scientific" than yours.

2. Below you'll find some of the "solutions" that naturalists have come up with to get around the idea of an eternal, self-existing, powerfully creative God. Are any of these natural solutions a better explanation than God? Can any of these hypotheses be proven, or are they based on an assumption—that is, are they granted as being true without being proven true (pages 106-108)?

Eternal, self-sufficient, creative force	Is this a better explanation than God? Is this assumed or proven?
The material world	
Multiverse generator	
Natural laws	
Light, quantum particles, quantum vacuums, etc.	

It's time to Roar Like a Mother at naturalism!

Recognize the Message

3. What are the two main messages of naturalism (page 109)?

Offer Discernment

4. Identify and explain one or more things that we can learn from

naturalism (that is, what truths does it offer, or what motives can we dignify)? List as many as you can think of, including those in the book.

5. Identify and explain the three lies that have been smuggled in with the partial truths of naturalism (pages 111-112).

Argue for a Healthier Approach

6. Choose one to three of the truths you identified above and interact with them. How does a balanced biblical approach achieve the goals

or affirm the truths that the proponents of naturalism are offering? Bonus points for scripture references!

a. What do you think is the proper relationship between science and faith?

b. In the Mama Bear Apologetics and Women in Apologetics statement of faith, we say, "Properly understood, God's Word (Scripture) and God's world (nature)...will never contradict each other." What do you think this means? What is the key phrase in this statement that cuts to the heart of perceived contradictions between God's natural revelation (nature) and His Scripture?

Reinforce Through Discussion, Discipleship, and Prayer

7. ROAR through one (or all) of the following scenarios:

a. You or your child are taking a class at a local college and the science teacher says in class, "Knowledge is acquired only through our natural senses, including taste, touch, smell, hearing, and sight. Because there is no God who has made Himself available to being detectable by our natural senses, we can state that God cannot be known." How, when, and where might you respond to your teacher?

b. Your child comes home from his or her first year in college and says science has conclusively shown that all we need is natural selection to create all the life forms we see on earth. What questions might you ask to help your child to identify the "eternal, uncaused, creative force" that he or she is now placing their faith in?

KEY SCRIPTURES

We encourage you to read the following verses in context (read at least the entire chapter), reflect on how they relate to what you're learning, and thank God for the hope and guidance found in His Word.

- *Job 12:7-10*—"Ask the beasts, and they will teach you; the birds of the heavens, and they will tell you; or the bushes of the earth, and they will teach you; and the fish of the sea will declare to you. Who among all these does not know that the hand of the LORD has done this? In his hand is the life of every living thing and the breath of all mankind."

- *Psalm 19:1*—"The heavens declare the glory of God, and the sky above proclaims his handiwork."

- *Romans 1:20*—"His invisible attributes, namely, his eternal power and divine nature, have been clearly perceived, ever since the creation of the world, in the things that have been made. So they are without excuse."

PAWS FOR PRAYER

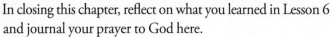

In closing this chapter, reflect on what you learned in Lesson 6 and journal your prayer to God here.

Praise:

Admit:

Worship with thanksgiving:

Supplication (ask):

I'D BELIEVE IN GOD IF THERE WERE ANY SHRED OF EVIDENCE—*SKEPTICISM*

In this chapter, we are not talking about healthy skepticism, but rather a radical hyper-skepticism that borders on cynicism. It's the kind of skepticism that refuses reasonable evidence and demands proof beyond a *possible* doubt (kind of like Ehrman was requesting). Absolute certainty can only be achieved in math and logic. With everything else, there is room for uncertainty. If people are wanting reasons to doubt Christianity, they'll find them. You can always put another question between yourself and God.

Mama Bear Apologetics, page 121

ACTIVE READING NOTES

READING FOCUS:	MY RESPONSE:
Before you read:	
After skimming the chapter title and subheads, what is one question you would like to have answered in the chapter?	My question:

While you read:	
Vocabulary: Here you will list three words *you* found in the chapter and a few words we want to make sure you found.	My words:
	Book words: *Hyper-skepticism* (page 121)—
After you read:	
Answer: Did you find an answer to your pre-reading question? (We hope so.) If yes, record it to the right.	My answer:
"Aha!" Moments: List three things you high-lighted or underlined in the chapter. This can be new information you learned or encouraging reinforcements of things you knew. Or just plain anything that popped out at you.	My "Aha!" moments: 1. 2. 3.

EMPOWERING WORDS

- *Faith*—Complete trust or strong belief in someone or something, loyalty backed by strong conviction. Biblically, the support for a believer's faith is based on the truths and facts found in Scripture.

- *Blind faith*—Beliefs or convictions that lack evidence or proof.

- *Skepticism*—An attitude of doubt or disbelief, the assertion that it's impossible to know something with certainty.

- *Empiricism*—The practice of relying strictly on the human senses or observations and experiments to obtain knowledge.

- *Dogmatism*—The strong expression of opinions as if they were facts even though the supporting evidence is questionable or insufficient.

- *Old atheist*—Person who defines atheism as the belief that "no God(s) exists"—literally "[a=no]theist."

- *New atheist*—Person (circa 2001 and later) who defines atheism as a "lack of God-belief." This reduces atheism from a propositional statement regarding *truth* (i.e., what does and does not exist in reality) to a propositional statement regarding a person's mental state regarding truth (i.e., main focus is on their personal belief, not on what exists in reality).

EMPOWERING THOUGHTS

There is a key difference between *proving* an idea and *supporting* an idea. Supporting a conclusion often involves multiple lines of evidence working together, without any one piece of evidence being fully conclusive on its own. But that's what the hyper-skeptic demands: a one-shot, single proof for Christianity. This person is looking for something as undeniable as 2 + 2 = 4. Historical evidence does not work that way, especially before video cameras! As we'll see, knowledge or evidence isn't the real problem for skeptics. Scripture says that "even the demons believe—and shudder!" (James 2:19).

DIGGING DEEPER

1. Chapter 7 of *Mama Bear Apologetics* opens with an account of the Daniel Wallace versus Bart Ehrman debate (pages 117-118). Ehrman explained the kind of evidence he would need to see before accepting that our modern-day translation of Mark's Gospel contains the exact wording as the original writings (i.e., the autographs).

   a. What evidence did Ehrman require (pages 117-119)?

b. Is that level of evidence realistic or reasonable? Why or why not (pages 118-119)?

c. What kinds of evidence do we have for the reliability of the Bible (page 119)?

2. Read the quote from David Hume on page 120 of *Mama Bear Apologetics*. This quote presents the "verifiability principle"—it is the principle Hume used to test whether something can be verified as true or false.

a. Does Hume's statement pass its own test of verifiability? Why or why not?

b. How might Hume's statement be self-defeating?

3. There are two types of skepticism mentioned in *Mama Bear Apologetics*. One type can lead to a more robust faith in God through

discipleship, and the other (in practice) prevents a person from believing anything at all.

    a. How does *Mama Bear Apologetics* define these two types of skepticism (pages 120-121)?

    b. How can understanding the difference help us navigate the doubts, questions, or skepticism expressed by our children?

> **It's time to Roar Like a Mother at skepticism!**

Recognize the Message

4. In your own words, what is skepticism (or more specifically, *hyper*-skepticism)?

5. Which four of the five messages of skepticism do you think are the most prevalent and why (pages 126-127)?

    —

    —

—

—

Offer Discernment

6. Identify and explain one or more things we can learn from skepticism (that is, what truths does it offer, or what motives can we dignify?). List as many as you can think of, including those in the book (pages 127-128).

7. What is the main lie that has snuck in with skepticism, making it go from a healthy skepticism to an unhealthy *hyper*-skepticism (page 128)?

Argue for a Healthier Approach

8. What is Christianity's "dirty little secret"? How does this apply to skepticism (page 129)?

9. Each of the main lies of skepticism identifies a legitimate concern (even if applied incorrectly). With the help of the passages listed below, how does Scripture address these problems skeptics have with Christianity?

    a. Religion is child abuse—read Proverbs 22:6; Ephesians 6:4; Hebrews 12:7-11

    b. Belief in God is like belief in Santa Claus—read John 16:33; Philippians 4:6-7; James 4:13-15

    c. Religion keeps people from asking questions—read Colossians 2:8; 1 Thessalonians 5:21; 1 John 4:1

Reinforce Through Discussion, Discipleship, and Prayer

10. Identify which of the following claims must be accepted with reasoned faith versus the ones that can be tested and supported with evidence. Some of these are tricky! (The answers and explanations are on pages 172-173, but no cheating!)

Claim	Faith or Evidence
The Bible was reliably transmitted.	
Believers are going to heaven.	
Jesus was a real person who lived, died, and rose again.	
Jesus's death means that we have eternal life.	
Sex outside of marriage is wrong.	
The only true knowledge is that which can be tested using the scientific method.	
God is good.	

11. Practice explaining the difference between *proof* and *support* to your kids. What examples could you provide of things that can be proven (page 121)?

12. Statements (or claims) are not evidence. What would you say to

your kids about how to discern the difference between a truth claim and a fact?

13. Activity: Pay attention to commercials on TV, radio, or in print (yes, that means not skipping through them on your DVR!), and practice asking these questions to your kids: What are some of the claims the advertisers make? Can these claims be tested? Are they even making a claim? Did the advertisement provide any data to back up its statement?

KEY SCRIPTURES

We encourage you to read the following verses in context (read at least the entire chapter), reflect on how they relate to what you're learning, and thank God for the hope and guidance found in His Word.

- *James 2:19*—"You believe that God is one; you do well. Even the demons believe—and shudder!"
- *John 12:37*—"Though he had done so many signs before them, they still did not believe in him."
- *Hebrews 11:1*—"Now faith is the assurance of things hoped for, the conviction of things not seen."

PAWS FOR PRAYER

In closing this chapter, reflect on what you learned in Lesson 7 and journal your prayer to God here.

Praise:

Admit:

Worship with thanksgiving:

Supplication (ask):

THE TRUTH IS, THERE IS NO TRUTH—*POSTMODERNISM*

Up until recently, our postmodern culture said that that *all* truth statements were in the subjective realm. We can't say, "Abortion is wrong." Rather, we can only say, "Abortion is wrong *for me.*" However, there is a world of difference between those statements.

Friend, as you talk with your children about important issues, you *must* understand this difference. When you tell them "Christianity is true," their postmodern mindset might be tacking on a silent "*for you*" at the end of that statement. When you say that something is true or right or wrong, they may agree *for now.* You might even see them dutifully nodding in agreement. However, if you don't get a handle on this postmodernism thing early, you might end up with a teenager or twenty-something who is completely respectful of all your "views." They are fine with those things being true *for you,* and not *for them.* If they have uncritically absorbed the lies of postmodernism, they will enter their young adult years trying to figure out "their truth" to build on, all the while being totally respectful of yours (until you try to claim that your truth should be theirs—then you'll have pushback).

Mama Bear Apologetics, pages 138-139

ACTIVE READING NOTES

READING FOCUS:	MY RESPONSE:
Before you read:	
After skimming the chapter title and subheads, what is one question you would like to have answered in the chapter?	My question:
While you read:	
Vocabulary: Here you will list three words *you* found in the chapter and a few words we want to make sure you found.	My words: Book words: *Worldview* (see page 45 in this study guide)— *Objective truth* (pages 137-138)— *Subjective truth* (page 138)— *Correspondence theory of truth* (page 143)—
After you read:	
Answer: Did you find an answer to your pre-reading question? (We hope so.) If yes, record it to the right.	My answer:

"*Aha!*" *Moments*:	My "Aha!" moments:
List three things you high-lighted or underlined in the chapter. This can be new information you learned or encouraging reinforcements of things you knew. Or just plain anything that popped out at you.	1. 2. 3.

EMPOWERING WORDS

- *Deconstructionism*—While there is no settled definition in philosophy, deconstruction is essentially taking apart a belief, worldview, or idea piece by piece, then question-ing each of the pieces to the point where the whole idea is finally dismissed.

- *Hyperfundamentalism*—A radical and unbiblical form of Christianity often characterized by extreme loyalty to movements or leaders, militant stances on nonessentials, inability to receive correction, and anti-intellectual bias. (Nowadays, people who use *fundamentalist* as a pejorative *mean* hyperfundamentalist.)

EMPOWERING THOUGHTS

If moms had a dollar for every question their children asked—even during one year of childhood—they would likely be able to retire the moment the nest was empty. It can be exhausting to answer all the pre-cious "Why, mommy?" and "What, mom?" questions we get during the growing-up years.

No matter how brain-straining our children's questions can be, why should we *not* stop the queries from coming (page 134)?

Postmodernism and Testimonies

One way postmodernism has impacted how Christians share their faith is the tendency to place heavy reliance on one's personal testimony. In the apostolic era, testimony for one's faith was largely centered on what people actually saw and heard that gave witness to Christ's life, death, resurrection, and deity. Today, however, our personal testimonies are filled with emotional highs and pragmatic stories of how Christianity has "worked" for us.

But what happens when the same personal "evidence" that we use for faith in Jesus (i.e., a changed life) can also be used by the followers of other world religions like Islam, Mormonism, Buddhism, or even nonreligious organizations like Alcoholics Anonymous? When personal testimony is used as the only source of evidence, it leaves no reliable way for others to evaluate whether that testimony is *true*.

Judaism and Christianity are the only religions that do not rely on private revelation alone. In the Old Testament, God performed His miracles in ways that made Him visible to all the nations. During the New Testament era, the life, death, and resurrection of Jesus occurred in a very public way, with many eyewitnesses available to vouch for the truthfulness of what had happened. The witness of the Holy Spirit *is* an important part of the testifying work of Christ to us as Christians, but it may not be persuasive to someone else.

DIGGING DEEPER

1. Read the quote from Nancy Pearcey on pages 135-136.

   a. What mistakes did our Christian forefathers make that may have helped contribute to the postmodern worldview?

   b. If there's *not* a God who created our brains, why should or shouldn't we trust human reasoning (page 136)?

2. On page 137, the authors state that "truth has become synonymous with _____ and _____."

3. How do you think this belief is affecting our claims that God and the Bible are *true*?

4. What is the difference between objective and subjective claims (page 138)?

5. According to postmodernism, truth and morality are subjective claims. What might be the consequences of your children absorbing a worldview that says truth and morality are subjective? How might that change the way you present truth and morality to your children (pages 138-139)?

It's time to Roar Like a Mother at postmodernism!

Recognize the Message

6. In your own words, what is postmodernism?

7. Which three of the four messages of postmodernism do you think are the most prevalent and why (pages 140-141)?

—

—

—

Offer Discernment

8. Identify and explain one or more things that we can learn from postmodernism—that is, what truths does it offer, or what motives can we dignify (pages 141-142)?

9. Identify and explain the three main lies that have been smuggled in with the partial truths of postmodernism (pages 143-144).

Argue for a Healthier Approach

10. As we discussed in the naturalism chapter, self-refuting statements make for a poor foundation. How can each of the lies listed above be turned on themselves?

Our perceptions determine reality—

All truth claims are power plays—

All truth is subjective—

11. Postmodernism is a reaction to hyperfundamentalism (which leaves no room for questioning even the smallest rules or traditions). Compare Romans 14:1-7 with 1 Corinthians 5:8-13. How can we rightly balance these two Scripture passages?

Reinforce Through Discussion, Discipleship, and Prayer

12. Read Alisa's story on page 144. How did she use cleverly worded questions to help her daughter discover for herself that absolute truth exists?

13. Let's play the objective versus subjective game! Challenge your kids to evaluate as many statements as possible and determine whether they are objective or subjective claims. And remember, advertisements are an *awesome* way to spot these kinds of statements. Below is a list of objective and subjective claims (and a few that are objective claims based on subjective information!). Identify the following as either objective or subjective. Add a few of your own at the end! See answers on page 174.

a. God exists—

b. Math is boring—

c. Stealing is wrong—

d. My brother is annoying—

e. There is no such thing as absolute truth—

f. My teacher hates me—

g. My example—

h. My example—

i. My example—

14. Your freshman in college comes home and states that the Bible was written mostly by white men and therefore cannot be trusted.

    a. What assumptions is your child making?

    b. How is postmodernism informing his or her statement? (Hint: see page 140.)

    c. How might you respond? (Hint: Step 1—*Was* the Bible written by white men? And even if it was, does that determine its truthfulness?)

KEY SCRIPTURES

We encourage you to read the following verses in context (read at least the entire chapter), reflect on how they relate to what you're learning—specifically with regard to truth—and thank God for the hope and guidance found in His Word.

- *2 Timothy 2:15*—"Do your best to present yourself to God as one approved, a worker who has no need to be ashamed, rightly handling the word of truth."
- *John 4:24*—"God is spirit, and those who worship him must worship in spirit and truth."
- *John 17:17*—"Sanctify them in the truth; your word is truth."
- *Proverbs 1:7*—"The fear of the LORD is the beginning of knowledge; fools despise wisdom and instruction."

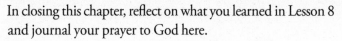

PAWS FOR PRAYER

In closing this chapter, reflect on what you learned in Lesson 8 and journal your prayer to God here.

Praise:

Admit:

Worship with thanksgiving:

Supplication (ask):

YOU'RE WRONG TO TELL ME THAT I'M WRONG—*MORAL RELATIVISM*

The *imago dei* is woven into our moral fabric. A person can say, "We can't judge other people's truths" all day long, but will get visibly uncomfortable when you ask if that applies to a hypothetical society that tortures babies for fun or believes that sex slavery is a solid business investment. Psychopaths aside, we *all* know that some things are wrong—for everyone, at all times, and in all cultures. The moral law is written on our hearts (Romans 2:15)...

Moral relativism says, "What's true for you may not be true for me. Nobody can tell me what is true. Let's all hold hands and sing 'Kumbaya.' Nobody is wrong—what's not to celebrate?" The *functional* conclusion, however, is just a new objective standard: Nobody can say that anybody else is wrong. If you do, you've broken the cardinal rule of moral relativism, and you will be publicly shamed for it.

Mama Bear Apologetics, page 155

ACTIVE READING NOTES

READING FOCUS:	MY RESPONSE:
Before you read:	
After skimming the chapter title and subheads, what is one question you would like to have answered in the chapter?	My question:
While you read:	
Vocabulary: Here you will list three words *you* found in the chapter and a few words we want to make sure you found.	My words: Book words: *Moral facts* (page 152)—
After you read:	
Answer: Did you find an answer to your pre-reading question? (We hope so.) If yes, record it to the right.	My answer:
"Aha!" Moments: List three things you highlighted or underlined in the chapter. This can be new information you learned or encouraging reinforcements of things you knew. Or just plain anything that popped out at you.	My "Aha!" moments: 1. 2. 3.

EMPOWERING WORDS

- *Moral relativism*—All moral truths are dependent on the moral judgments of a person's mind (that is, subjective experience, feelings, opinions, beliefs). These judgments will vary across different peoples and cultures.

- *Imago dei*—Literally "the image of God." As God's image bearers, even though we are fallen sinners, we still have the *imago dei* built into us.

- *Relative*—In comparison to or in relation to something else.

- *Absolute*—Totally certain, with no ifs, ands, or buts.

- *Morality*—The standard or code by which people determine what is good/right or bad/wrong (and which assumes that we already know what is good and right).

- *Metaphysics*—Branch of philosophy that deals with the nature of reality, how we know reality, and "first principles," which are fundamental assumptions that must be granted without scientific experimentation.

EMPOWERING THOUGHTS

In the movie *Frozen II,* Anna sings a song about doing the "next right thing." When we talk about moral values, we are talking about whether something is *good* or *bad*. When we talk about moral duties, we are talking about whether something is *right* or *wrong*. It is generally accepted that it is *good* to do *right* things and *wrong* to do *bad* things.

This is where linguistic theft becomes highly important. If we redefine what is meant by the concepts of good or bad, that automatically changes how a person decides what is the *right* thing to do!

Below is a list of beliefs about what is *good* that will radically change what the *right* thing to do is. Based on the belief, what might someone determine is the "next right thing"?

Belief	"Next Right Thing"
I deserve happiness and to feel good about myself.	*Example: Do anything that makes you feel better about yourself, even if it involves hurting other people.*
Personal and sexual fulfillment are the most important aspects of a marriage.	
It is bad to say anything that makes someone uncomfortable.	
It is bad to have a child when you are not ready for one.	
It is good to affirm that all beliefs can be equally true, depending on the person.	
It is bad (inauthentic) to change your behavior if the change doesn't come naturally.	

DIGGING DEEPER

1. What is the biggest problem with society thinking that we can create our own morals (that is, basically make our own rules) (page 149)?

2. How do moral relativism and the new definition of tolerance ultimately conflict with one another (pages 150-151)?

3. "Emotions are now the main arbiters of moral truth. The *strength* of one's emotions determines exactly *how* right or wrong something is" (page 151). How have you seen this statement played out in society?

4. How does the story *The Portrait of Dorian Grey* illustrate the concept of breaking the moral law (page 152)? How did Oscar Wilde depict the consequences of breaking the moral law?

5. Below is a sampling of moral tools in our toolbox. How can using *just this one tool to the exclusion of all the others* be harmful? (Side note: We are not claiming that Scripture alone is insufficient for knowing truth.)

Tool Used by Itself	Possible Negative Side Effects
Example: Scripture	*Example: People never teach their kids or new converts **why** they believe what they believe, only **what** to believe. Or they fail to exercise compassion on someone who is hurting from sin.*
Compassion	
Absolute truth	

Love	
Tolerance	

6. How would using all these tools together help us to be most effective in proclaiming Christ?

7. Read Romans 2:15 and answer the following questions (see also pages 154-156).

    a. Can people know basic moral laws without having read the Bible or getting special revelation from God? Explain.

    b. Can people know basic moral laws but not realize they know them?

8. Explain the new "Frankenstein of religion" that our kids are being bullied into having (page 156).

It's time to Roar Like a Mother at moral relativism!

Recognize the Message

9. In your own words, what is moral relativism?

10. Which four of the five messages of moral relativism do you think are the most prevalent, and why (pages 156-157)?

—

—

—

—

Offer Discernment

11. Identify and explain one or more things that we can learn from moral relativism (that is, what truths does it offer, or what motives can we dignify)? List as many as you can think of, including those in the book.

12. Identify and explain which three of the four lies smuggled in with moral relativism you think are the most prevalent, and why (pages 158-159).

Argue for a Healthier Approach

13. Which five of the six suggestions for combatting moral relativism do you think are the most important for your children to understand, and why?

—

—

—

—

—

Reinforce Through Discussion, Discipleship, and Prayer

14. Your daughter comes home from summer camp and says she was taught that no real Christian woman would ever wear a two-piece bathing suit.

  a. Do you agree or disagree? Why?

  b. How do you help her ROAR through this statement?

15. The Bible and Beer Consortium (BBC) (www.thebibleandbeer consortium.com) was created to bring atheists and Christians together in an atheist-friendly environment. The BBC brings Christian speakers from all over the world to give lectures on theological and cultural topics and to engage in collegial debates with skeptics.

a. What are some biblical examples for or against using this type of platform for reaching the lost?

b. Is this avenue of outreach a good idea for every Christian to participate in? Why or why not?

KEY SCRIPTURES

We encourage you to read the following verses in context (read at least the entire chapter), reflect on how they relate to what you're learning, and thank God for the hope and guidance found in His Word.

- *Proverbs 14:12*—"There is a way that seems right to a man, but its end is the way to death."

- *Romans 1:18-20*—"The wrath of God is revealed from heaven against all ungodliness and unrighteousness of men, who by their unrighteousness suppress the truth. For what can be known about God is plain to them, because God has shown it to them. For by his invisible attributes, namely, his eternal power and divine nature, have been clearly perceived, ever since the creation of the world, in the things that have been made. So they are without excuse."

- *Romans 2:15*—"They show that the work of the law is written on their hearts, while their conscience also bears witness, and their conflicting thoughts accuse or even excuse them."

- Judges 17:6—"In those days there was no king in Israel. Everyone did what was right in his own eyes."

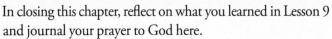

PAWS FOR PRAYER

In closing this chapter, reflect on what you learned in Lesson 9 and journal your prayer to God here.

Praise:

Admit:

Worship with thanksgiving:

Supplication (ask):

FOLLOW YOUR HEART—IT NEVER LIES!—*EMOTIONALISM*

The problem with using our emotions for determining truth is that they have to first be *conformed to truth* in order to tell us anything useful. For a compass to work, it must first be magnetized. Otherwise, it won't point to true north. Disciplining our emotions with truth is like magnetizing our emotional compass. We can follow our emotions, but only *after* we have made sure our emotional compass is pointing in the right direction.

Too many people today determine truth by their emotions yet have not bothered to magnetize their emotional compasses. They say, "Let's go north!" and proceed to walk in all different directions, trying to convince everyone else to follow them. Instead of disciplining their emotions to match reality, they are trying to make reality match their emotions. When they feel scared, they *assume* that they are in danger—instead of perceiving real danger and then feeling scared. In this way, emotionalism mistakes feelings for facts. But there's little assurance that those emotion-loaded opinions are indeed *facts* unless Scripture, reason, and reality are fact-checking those feelings. And when people have already bought into postmodernism, then they don't even believe that they *can* know objective truth. One person's feeling can be just as "factual" as the next—which is to say, none of us have the facts and we're all wandering lost in a maze of wrong.

Mama Bear Apologetics, pages 171-172

ACTIVE READING NOTES

READING FOCUS:	MY RESPONSE:
Before you read:	
After skimming the chapter title and subheads, what is one question you would like to have answered in the chapter?	My question:
While you read:	
Vocabulary: Here you will list three words *you* found in the chapter and a few words we want to make sure you found.	My words: Book words: *Passions* (page 169)— *Emotions* (page 169)—
After you read:	
Answer: Did you find an answer to your pre-reading question? (We hope so.) If yes, record it to the right.	My answer:

"Aha!" Moments:	My "Aha!" moments:
List three things you highlighted or underlined in the chapter. This can be new information you learned or encouraging reinforcements of things you knew. Or just plain anything that popped out at you.	1. 2. 3.

EMPOWERING WORDS

- *Reason*—The ability of the mind to think, understand, and support thoughts and conclusions through logic.

- *Reality*—The way things actually are, the state in which they exist.

- *Judgment*—Assessing a situation and drawing conclusions based on one's perception of truth.

EMPOWERING THOUGHTS

Twenty-five. According to science, that's the number of years it takes for the prefrontal cortex in the brain to fully develop. With this in mind, we can see just how important it is that we are able to discern the difference between a healthy emotional life and emotionalism. The first is an aspect of well-rounded living. The other is a dangerous and fickle driver on the roads of life.

What do you think is the difference between healthy emotions and emotionalism?

DIGGING DEEPER

1. Read "The Difference Between Emotions and Passions" (pages 168-170), and then answer the following:

   a. How do the authors and Robert Solomon describe the difference between emotions and passions?

   b. "Well-informed emotions can strengthen your grasp on truth" (page 169). What does this mean?

2. How are emotions like a compass (page 171)?

3. Read "A Brief History of Emotionalism" (pages 170-172) and answer the following questions:

   a. What exactly is emotionalism?

   b. How might those with a postmodern mindset be vulnerable to the consequences of emotionalism?

   c. How does emotionalism leave us vulnerable to bad theology and a wrong understanding of what the Bible says?

It's time to Roar Like a Mother at emotionalism!

Recognize the Message

4. Emotionalism is different from the other ROAR topics we've examined in that we need to recognize the message by understanding the *assumptions* behind the message, and the way the message is packaged. (This one's a sneaky little devil!)

Describe the first two assumptions. How do they necessarily lead to the third assumption (pages 172-173)?

a. Assumption 1:

b. Assumption 2:

c. How do these lead to assumption 3?

5. What are some examples of ways you've seen emotionalism evident under the following labels?

a. Trigger warnings (page 174)—

  b. Follow your heart (page 174)—

  c. I'm offended (page 175)—

Offer Discernment

6. List as many positives/pros and negatives/cons as you can for emotions.

Emotions—Pros/positives	Emotions—Cons/negatives

Offer Discernment

7. Identify and explain one or more things we can learn from emotionalism (that is, what truths does it offer, or what motives can we dignify?). List as many as you can think of, including those in the book.

8. Identify and explain the three lies smuggled in with emotionalism. How does the third lie logically follow the first two (pages 176-178)?

—

—

—

Argue for a Healthier Approach

9. What is the difference between truth and a truth *claim* (page 178)?

10. What can you do to help your children "take captive every thought" (2 Corinthians 10:5)? More specifically, from pages 179-180:

11. In what ways can you help your children realize they can exercise control over their emotions?

12. How can you affirm your children when their emotions do align with truth?

Reinforce Through Discussion, Discipleship, and Prayer

13. Answer the following questions, preferably with your own examples (pages 180-182). How can children be taught to...

a. recognize different emotions in themselves?

b. recognize different emotions in others?

c. exercise control over their emotions?

d. integrate emotions into their decision-making?

14. Your child is having a birthday party and wants to invite most of his/her class except one girl who is known to have poor hygiene and not many friends. All the other kids think she is weird and make fun of her. Take your child through the Z-model for decision-making so she can determine whether to invite this one girl to the birthday party.

15. Your teenage daughter struggles with insecurity and feelings of worthlessness. She has been a Christian for many years now, active in her youth group, and by all evidences, truly loves the Lord. She can tell you when she first put her faith in Christ and asked Him to be her Lord and Savior. One day, she confesses to you that she's not sure whether she's really saved. When you ask her why she thinks that, she tells you that she just doesn't feel God's love; He seems distant, like He's forsaken her.

a. How might emotionalism be affecting your daughter's faith, and which lie (pages 176-178) is she believing?

b. How would you counsel your daughter?

KEY SCRIPTURES

We encourage you to read the following verses in context (read at least the entire chapter), reflect on how they relate to what you're learning, and thank God for the hope and guidance found in His Word.

- *Jeremiah 17:9*—"The heart is deceitful above all things, and desperately sick; who can understand it?"

- *Romans 12:2*—"Be transformed by the renewal of your mind, that by testing you may discern what is the will of God, what is good and acceptable and perfect."

- *Luke 10:27*—"He answered, 'You shall love the Lord your God with all your heart and with all your soul and with all your strength and with all your mind, and your neighbor as yourself.'"

- *2 Corinthians 10:5*—"We destroy arguments and every lofty opinion raised against the knowledge of God, and take every thought captive to obey Christ."

PAWS FOR PRAYER

In closing this chapter, reflect on what you learned in Lesson 10 and journal your prayer to God here.

Praise:

Admit:

Worship with thanksgiving:

Supplication (ask):

JUST WORSHIP
SOMETHING—*PLURALISM*

Pluralism, by definition, refers to a society with ethnic, racial, religious, social, and ideological diversity. But for our purposes, we want to discuss *religious* pluralism, the idea that all religions offer legitimate paths to God. It's not just that many people have different religious ideas, but that they make truth claims (even contradicting ones) and assert they are *equally valid*...

In a society where multiple religious beliefs coexist, *secularism, colored with tolerance, leads to the false dichotomy that either (1) all religions are equally valid, or (2) no religion should be discussed.* There is no middle ground. You must either affirm all religions or acknowledge none of them.

Mama Bear Apologetics, pages 186-187

ACTIVE READING NOTES

READING FOCUS:	MY RESPONSE:
Before you read:	
After skimming the chapter title and subheads, what is one question you would like to have answered in the chapter?	My question:

While you read:	
Vocabulary: Here you will list three words *you* found in the chapter and a few words we want to make sure you found.	My words:
	Book words:
	Religious pluralism (page 186)—
	Secularism (page 187)—
	Tolerance (from a secularist perspective, page 187)—
	Tolerance (from a correct perspective, pages 70 and 187)—
	Law of non-contradiction (page 190)—
After you read:	
Answer: Did you find an answer to your pre-reading question? (We hope so.) If yes, record it to the right.	My answer:

"Aha!" Moments:	My "Aha!" moments:
List three things you high-lighted or underlined in the chapter. This can be new information you learned or encouraging reinforcements of things you knew. Or just plain anything that popped out at you.	1. 2. 3.

EMPOWERING WORDS

- *Inclusivism*—Holds that differing sets of beliefs are true and valid.

- *Exclusivism*—Asserts that only one way is true, and all other ways are in error.

- *Politically correct*—Avoiding words, viewpoints, or actions that are considered uncomfortable or offensive to certain categories of people. As word meanings and ideas are hijacked, the definition of what is offensive can change according to progressive thinking.

- *Truth claim*—The assertion that a specific belief is true; thus anything contradictory to that claim cannot be true.

EMPOWERING THOUGHTS

There is a huge difference between tolerating *people* and tolerating *bad ideas*. At Mama Bear Apologetics, we say to demolish arguments, not people. What does Scripture say about how we should act when we discuss the differences between Christianity and other belief systems?

Ephesians 4:15—

2 Timothy 2:24-25—

Titus 3:2—

1 Peter 3:15—

Lie #4 of pluralism (see pages 192-193 in *Mama Bear Apologetics*) is that the true gospel unites all people. The word *unity* most often has a positive connotation, but in reality, unity is neither morally good nor bad. If we have unity with righteousness, that is good. If, however, we unify with evil, that's not good. We must be careful not to unite solely for unity's sake. The Bible instructs us to be in unity with other like-minded believers. Read the Mama Bear blog post titled "Teaching Our Kids to Spot Empty Statements" at https://mamabearapologetics.com /empty-message-unity/ and consider the following quote: "The problem with unity is that it *implies* division. In order to unify over one thing, you have to divide from its opposite."

While we cannot judge what is in someone else's heart, how can we discern whether we should unify with someone?

How can we reflect God's love to nonbelievers without unifying with them?

DIGGING DEEPER

It's time to Roar Like a Mother at pluralism!

Recognize the Message

1. In your own words, what is pluralism?

2. Why is the simple message of the popular bumper sticker COEXIST so appealing (see page 188)? Explain why CONTRADICT might be a more fitting bumper sticker.

3. How has the "pursuit of peace" caused people to be silent about the gospel? How have some Christians replaced the gospel (sin, repentance, and God's free gift of salvation through grace) so that they don't risk offending anyone (page 188)?

Offer Discernment

4. In what ways we can show love to our neighbors (who may have differing beliefs) without affirming their beliefs (page 189)?

5. Identify and explain which three of the four lies smuggled in with pluralism you think are the most prevalent, and why (pages 189-192).

Argue for a Healthier Approach

6. In what ways does the story of Daniel illustrate how we are to live in a pagan culture (pages 193-195)?

7. Why do we sometimes find it difficult to proclaim that Jesus is

the only way to God and, at the same time, build earnest, loving connections with people of other faiths?

8. What are some steps we can take to overcome this difficulty?

Reinforce Through Discussion, Discipleship, and Prayer

9. Is your child able to explain, in very clear, simple terms, what it takes for a person to receive Christ as Lord and Savior? Take some time to walk through the following Bible verses together, and have your child explain, in his or her own words, the path to salvation in Christ, which, as John 14:6 says, is the only way to God.

- Romans 3:10-11,23
- Romans 6:23
- Romans 5:12
- Romans 10:9

10. A good way to help children understand the significance of Christ's proclamation "I am the way, and the truth, and the life" (John 14:6) is to pick a different religion and examine what that religion teaches about sin, salvation, the way to heaven, and Christ's identity as God. Choose a religion you would like to investigate, identifying each of these aspects. On a sheet of paper, list some of the basic differences between what the Bible teaches and what the other religion teaches. Help your children identify which contradictory claims cannot both be true at the same time. We

recommend starting with Lindsey Medenwaldt's series on the Mama Bear Apologetics blog.

11. Talk to your children about different types of buildings—different houses, museums, restaurants, etc. What would they say if someone were to tell them that all the buildings were "basically the same" because they all have windows, a floor, a roof, and some of the same building materials? How might you compare this to the claim that all religions are basically the same?

KEY SCRIPTURES

We encourage you to read the following verses in context (read at least the entire chapter), reflect on how they relate to what you're learning, and thank God for the hope and guidance found in His Word.

- *John 14:6*—"I am the way, and the truth, and the life. No one comes to the Father except through me."

- *Isaiah 45:5-6*—"I am the LORD, and there is no other, besides me there is no God; I equip you, though you do not know me, that people may know, from the rising of the sun and from the west, that there is none besides me; I am the LORD, and there is no other."

- *Romans 1:19-20*—"What can be known about God is plain to them, because God has shown it to them. For his invisible attributes, namely, his eternal power and divine nature, have been clearly perceived, ever since the creation of the world, in the things that have been made. So they are without excuse."

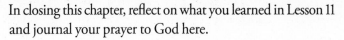

PAWS FOR PRAYER

In closing this chapter, reflect on what you learned in Lesson 11 and journal your prayer to God here.

Praise:

Admit:

Worship with thanksgiving:

Supplication (ask):

I'M NOT RELIGIOUS; I'M SPIRITUAL—*NEW SPIRITUALITY*

By 2012, Pew Research Center reported that one-third of millennials don't ascribe to any particular religion, with 37% of that group describing themselves as "spiritual but not religious," and 58% feeling "a deep connection with nature and the earth." Combine that with major celebrities telling them to "live their truth," and you've got fertile soil for New Age doctrines to take root under the guise of what's now called the new spirituality.

This new spirituality is just good ol' New Age with a modern makeover. It has shed the image of a fortune teller wielding a crystal ball and has now been refashioned in the image of a hipster wearing skinny jeans...wielding a latte...and often wearing a cross. Same message, different branding.

Mama Bear Apologetics, page 201

ACTIVE READING NOTES

READING FOCUS:	MY RESPONSE:
Before you read:	
After skimming the chapter title and subheads, what is one question you would like to have answered in the chapter?	My question:

While you read:	
Vocabulary: Here you will list three words *you* found in the chapter and a few words we want to make sure you found.	My words: Book words: *Pantheism* (pages 202-203)— *Transcendence* (page 207)—
After you read:	
Answer: Did you find an answer to your pre-reading question? (We hope so.) If yes, record it to the right.	My answer:
"Aha!" Moments: List three things you high-lighted or underlined in the chapter. This can be new information you learned or encouraging reinforcements of things you knew. Or just plain anything that popped out at you.	My "Aha!" moments: 1. 2. 3.

EMPOWERING WORDS

- *New Age*—Religious and spiritual beliefs that grew rapidly in the 1970s and drew its practices from occult traditions. New Age emphasizes a person's experiences and self-knowledge as the primary sources of revelation and truth. It incorporates many traditions and terminology from world religions like Buddhism, Hinduism, and Christianity without itself being committed to any one tradition.

- *Occult*—Literally means "hidden," but carries the connotation of pursuing knowledge through supernatural or magical means.

- *Mysticism*—Revelation of hidden or ultimate spiritual knowledge which is accessed through a religiously induced altered state of consciousness rather than rational thought.

- *Theism*—Belief that God exists.

- *Monotheism*—Belief that only one God exists.

- *Christ consciousness*—The belief that Jesus Christ was a man like us who, after realizing His innate divinity, was able to perform godlike acts. Only when we realize our own divinity can we truly imitate Christ and perform the same acts as He.

EMPOWERING THOUGHTS

A major theme within new spirituality (and self-helpism!) is an emphasis on recognizing your "true self." According to new spirituality, our challenge is that we don't know ourselves well enough, and our problems can only be overcome when we fully understand our true natures and reclaim our identities. Is knowing yourself a bad thing? Absolutely not. Does it help you identify weaknesses in yourself? Sure. Does it do *anything* to fix those weaknesses? NO.

In what ways have you noticed an overemphasis on "knowing yourself" creeping into the church?

DIGGING DEEPER

1. What is NAM? Explain what the acronym stands for and define a few of its influences (pages 200-201).

2. What are some examples of New Age/new spirituality that are present in popular culture (pages 199-202)?

3. Review pages 201-202. In the book *A Course in Miracles,* author and Columbia University professor Helen Schucman records her collection of spiritual revelations from "the Voice," whom she later identifies as Jesus. Read the six "revelations" on page 202 and imagine the author is making these truth claims to you directly. In the space below, write your reply to each one. In your responses, consider what these claims would take away from your walk with Jesus—how things would change for you. We'll do the first "revelation" for you:

   a. "Do not make the pathetic error of 'clinging to the old rugged cross.' The only message of the crucifixion is that you can overcome the cross."
   Response: *It's not pathetic at all to cling to the old rugged cross. That cross is everything to me. It represents the deepest love, the greatest forgiveness, the purest hope. Nothing else I've ever tried has washed me as clean as the blood shed on that beautiful cross.*

Reply to the remaining five claims:

   b. "The name of Jesus Christ as such is but a symbol. But it stands for love that is not of this world. It is a symbol that is safely used as a replacement for the many names of all the gods to which you pray."

Response:

c. "The Atonement is the final lesson he need learn, for it teaches him that, never having sinned, he has no need of salvation."

Response:

d. Lesson 61 asks the reader to affirm "I am the light of the world."

Response:

e. Lesson 259 asks the reader to affirm "there is no sin."

Response:

f. Lesson 70 ask the reader to affirm "my salvation comes from me."

Response:

4. There are some teachings creeping into Christianity that tell you to just empty your mind, ask the Lord to speak, and then record whatever you hear, trusting that it is from God. This is exactly what Helen Schucman did. Do you think her messages were from God? Why or why not?

5. The belief that God is all and all is one is called *pantheism* (pages 202-203, 207).

     a. How does this view compare with Christian monotheism?

     b. What are some things you enjoy about your relationship with God that would be lost with pantheism?

6. New spirituality teaches that you and I are either an extension of God or our own little gods (pages 204-205). Why might this idea be attractive to people?

It's time to Roar Like a Mother at new spirituality!

Recognize the Message

7. Describe the four main emphases of New Age mysticism/new spirituality:

a. Pantheism:

b. Divinity of all mankind:

c. Relativism:

d. Meditation:

8. How does creation point us toward God, according to Romans 1:19-20?

9. Is that the same thing as creation *being* God? Why or why not?

10. Relativism can sound like a tolerant way to accept other people's beliefs. What are some ways that true relativism conflicts with reality (pages 208-209)?

Offer Discernment

11. What are some specific *motivations* within new spirituality that we can affirm (page 207)?

12. How should a Christian respond to each of the messages within new spirituality? Are there any partial truths found within these?

a. Pantheism:

b. Divinity of all mankind:

c. Relativism:

d. Meditation:

13. Transcendental Meditation aims to empty one's mind or turn off lucid thought by focusing on a phrase or word (a mantra) until rational discernment dissolves and the individual becomes a passive receptor for the spiritual realm. How is this different from biblical meditation as described in the following verses (pages 206-207)?

   a. Psalm 1:1-2—

   b. Psalm 77:12—

   c. Philippians 4:8—

14. What warnings does Scripture give us about seeking spiritual

insight apart from God's Word (see 2 Corinthians 11:14; 1 Timothy 4:1)?

Argue for a Healthier Approach

15. Compared to what new spirituality teaches, how does Scripture paint a more realistic version of mankind *and* solve our ultimate problem?

Reinforce Through Discussion, Discipleship, and Prayer

16. Suppose one of your friends is a new Christian who used to be very involved with NAM. She is eager to take the practices she learned during her New Age days and "use them to the glory of God." How do you respond?

17. Your daughter is a strong Christian. She tells you that after fasting and praying, she asked to hear from the Lord and received answers by engaging in automatic writing (automatic writing is where a person is not writing their own conscious thoughts, but allowing their hand to write supposedly subconscious thoughts or thoughts channeled from the spiritual realm). Your daughter's writing includes all sorts of Bible verses backing up the statements, but also contains several *themes*

that contradict with Scripture in its full context. She is certain that because she asked to hear from the Lord, everything she wrote is from Him. How do you respond? (By the way, this is based on a true story.)

KEY SCRIPTURES

We encourage you to read the following verses in context (read at least the entire chapter), reflect on how they relate to what you're learning, and thank God for the hope and guidance found in His Word.

- *2 Timothy 4:3-4*—"The time is coming when people will not endure sound teaching, but having itching ears they will accumulate for themselves teachers to suit their own passions, and will turn away from listening to the truth and wander off into myths."

- *John 8:23*—"He said to them, 'You are from below; I am from above. You are of this world; I am not of this world.'"

- *Deuteronomy 29:29*—"The secret things belong to the LORD our God, but the things that are revealed belong to us and to our children forever, that we may do all the words of this law."

PAWS FOR PRAYER

In closing this chapter, reflect on what you learned in Lesson 12 and journal your prayer to God here.

Praise:

Admit:

Worship with thanksgiving:

Supplication (ask):

COMMUNISM FAILED BECAUSE NOBODY DID IT RIGHT—*MARXISM*

Just so no one misunderstands me, I want to say right now that *the Bible is not pro-capitalism and America is not God's chosen nation*. I am not trying to make a statement on political parties here. Rather, my goal is to expose the lies that are being smuggled into our children's minds through Marxism. Marxist ideas in the form of socialism and communism can *sound* completely reasonable, and even gospel-driven. But make no mistake: The end goal is the dissolution of all hierarchies. And yes, that includes the family unit, religion, and morality. Marx says in *The Communist Manifesto*, "Communism is that stage of historical development which makes all existing religions superfluous and supersedes them" and that "Communism abolishes eternal truths, it abolishes all religion, and all morality." He even refers to the sacredness of the relationship between parent and child as "disgusting."

Marxism is more than just a failed economic policy—it is essentially a religion, one that touches on every facet of life from church to family to morality.

Mama Bear Apologetics, pages 216-217

ACTIVE READING NOTES

READING FOCUS:	MY RESPONSE:
Before you read:	
After skimming the chapter title and subheads, what is one question you would like to have answered in the chapter?	My question:
While you read:	
Vocabulary: Here you will list three words *you* found in the chapter and a few words we want to make sure you found.	My words: Book words: *Capitalism* (page 221)— *Marxism* (page 218)— *Socialism* (page 218)— *Communism* (page 218)—
After you read:	
Answer: Did you find an answer to your pre-reading question? (We hope so.) If yes, record it to the right.	My answer:

"Aha!" Moments:	My "Aha!" moments:
List three things you highlighted or underlined in the chapter. This can be new information you learned or encouraging reinforcements of things you knew. Or just plain anything that popped out at you.	1. 2. 3.

EMPOWERING WORDS

- *Ends justify the means*—A positive outcome can justify the methods one takes to achieve it, even if the methods are unethical.

- *Secularism*—A philosophy that seeks to interpret life based on principles taken solely from the material world (secular, not religious).

- *Humanism*—A belief system that stresses human potential and goodness and seeks solely rational ways of solving human problems—of prime importance is the human rather than the divine.

EMPOWERING THOUGHTS

Prior to 1980, kids were taught all the best parts of American history—the bravery of our foreparents, their fearless search for religious freedom, etc. In 1980, Howard Zinn published a book titled *The People's History of the United States*, in which he rewrote much of American history and claimed that the founding of America was motivated largely by greed and the pursuit of power. The truth is probably somewhere in between, for most moments in history are full of both good and evil motives. Why? Because history is the record of *people*. Fallen people.

On page 216 of *Mama Bear Apologetics*, we read, "Those who are ignorant of history are doomed to repeat it." How does looking at *only* the good or the bad taint the lessons we can learn from history? Why is it important to recognize both the good and bad?

How does the Bible objectively record the history of Israel and the early church without rose-colored *or* dirt-colored glasses?

Marx taught that all differences between people were reduced to economic inequalities—the literal haves versus the have-nots. The modern Marxist teaches that all differences between people are due to inequalities of *power*. For these problems to be addressed, the oppressed class needs to revolt against the so-called oppressor class. Read Matthew 5:38-44 and 6:19-24. How does being a Christ-follower address the concerns that Marxists have regarding both money and power?

Read 1 Corinthians 1:27. How does God's economy flip all these fights regarding money and power upside down?

DIGGING DEEPER

1. Read the section titled "Why Are We Talking About Failed Economic Policies in a Book for Moms?" on pages 216-217.

a. What are some of the ideas and concepts that Marxism is trying to dissolve or abolish?

b. Why should this concern us? (That is, how would dissolving or abolishing the ideas and concepts listed above hinder our ability to practice Christianity and raise healthy families?)

2. Read pages 219-220 and answer the following:

a. What critical factor about humans does Marx ignore?

b. How does missing the original problem (sin) affect the way a person determines the solution?

c. What do Marxists think needs to happen in order to make evil people good?

3. Let's turn our attention now to what the Bible teaches about the origin of evil.

   a. According to a biblical worldview, what has gone wrong with humanity? In other words, what does the Bible say about the origin of evil (see John 8:44; Romans 5:12; Ephesians 6:12)?

   b. How does the Marxist solution for humanity's evil differ from the Bible's solution?

4. Explain the "ends justify the means" mentality. What are some of the potential consequences of this ideology (page 220)?

5. On page 221, we mention two legitimate wrongs that *The Communist Manifesto* brought to light. How might recognizing this alter the way you feel about reading literature with which you might normally disagree or avoid?

It's time to Roar Like a Mother at Marxism!

Recognize the Message

6. Which four of the five messages of Marxism do you think are the most prevalent, and why (pages 223-225)?

—

—

—

—

Offer Discernment

7. Identify and explain one or more things that we can learn from social justice warriors (that is, what truths do they offer, or what motives can we dignify?). List as many as you can think of, including those in the book.

8. Why should we be careful about the way we critique social justice warriors (pages 226-227)?

9. Identify and explain at least four of the seven lies you think are most prevalent that have been smuggled in with the partial truths of Marxism (pages 227-230).

—

—

—

—

Argue for a Healthier Approach

10. Choose one to three of the truths you identified above and interact with them. How does a balanced biblical approach achieve the goals or affirm the truths that the proponents of Marxism are offering? Bonus points for scripture references!

11. What does the Bible say about how we are to respond to injustice (see Psalms 82:3; Proverbs 21:3; Isaiah 1:17; Matthew 23:23)?

Reinforce Through Discussion, Discipleship, and Prayer

12. At first glance, it can be difficult to tell the difference between a Marxist cause and a biblical cause. This is because both use the same words (specifically the ones mentioned in the linguistic theft chapter, plus *sexist, racist, oppression,* and more). Because most people ignorantly assume we're all on the same page—especially when it comes to big ideas such as *love, freedom,* and *justice*—a lot of miscommunication takes place. As the saying goes, "The devil is in the [hidden] details."

Our goal is to help our children recognize these *category* words and learn to ask clarifying questions almost as quickly as they say "Mine!" when you try to take a cookie from them. A great question to ask our children is this: "What specifically do you mean by (insert buzzword here)?"

Activity 1: Buzzwords Board

Create a "buzzwords board" together with age-appropriate words like *deserve, justice, equality, oppression, racism, sexism, homophobic*, etc. As you go about your day, listen for the buzzwords and use the board to help identify when a buzzword is being used to describe a *specific action* as opposed to when it is being used to vilify a person or cause without giving any details.

When your children hear a buzzword being used, teach them to immediately ask, "What actually happened here?" If they can't get a satisfactory answer, that's likely a sign that the word is being held hostage by linguistic theft. (By the way, special thanks to Sarah Savick for this idea!)

Activity 2: Identifying Marxism in Mission Statements

The book *Rules for Radicals* is the modern playbook for the social justice movement and is laced with a heavy dose of Marxism. In it, Saul Alinsky's thesis statement reads, "My aim here is to suggest how to organize for power: how to get it and how to use it" ([New York: Vintage Books, 1989], 10). Later, he gives many of his rules for engagement, such as "do what you can with what you have and *clothe it in moral language*" (page 36, emphasis added). Thus, many Marxist agendas take a legitimate grievance and then shoehorn in a bunch of other political policies, like gun control, demilitarizing the police, prison reform, LGBTQ+ issues, and more.

When you have time, go to www.womensmarch.com, click on "About," and then "Mission and Principles." Scroll down until you see "Download Unity Principles" and click on it. Print out the document and mark it up in the following way: Draw a circle around every issue that is phrased in moral language but doesn't include details as to what the phrase means. Grab two different highlighter pens and with one color, highlight every issue that you believe is a legitimate women's issue that should be addressed. With the other color, highlight every issue that either (1) has nothing to do with women or (2) is not exclusive to women. How have these ideas been shoehorned with a legitimate grievance? (Hint: Between ages 8-12, kids will be able to start differentiating black and white areas from grey areas. Attempting this exercise with kids who are younger than this will be difficult. If your children have the attention span and intellectual capacity to do this with you, then go ahead. If they don't, then mark the document first, and then discuss it together.)

KEY SCRIPTURES

We encourage you to read the following verses in context (read at least the entire chapter), reflect on how they relate to what you're learning, and thank God for the hope and guidance found in His Word.

- *Galatians 3:26-28*—"In Christ Jesus you are all sons of God, through faith. For as many of you as were baptized into Christ have put on Christ. There is neither Jew nor Greek, there is neither slave nor free, there is no male and female, for you are all one in Christ Jesus."

- *James 1:27*—"Religion that is pure and undefiled before God the Father is this: to visit orphans and widows in their affliction, and to keep oneself unstained from the world."

- *Romans 3:9-12*—"What then? Are we Jews any better off? No, not at all. For we have already charged that all, both Jews and Greeks, are under sin, as it is written: 'None is righteous, no, not one; no one understands; no one seeks for God. All have turned aside; together they have become worthless; no one does good, not even one.'"

PAWS FOR PRAYER

In closing this chapter, reflect on what you learned in Lesson 13 and journal your prayer to God here.

Praise:

Admit:

Worship with thanksgiving:

Supplication (ask):

THE FUTURE IS FEMALE—*FEMINISM*

Don't get us wrong. Like all dutiful daughters of modernity, we're thankful for feminism. And as Christians, we are thankful for a God who gave woman-honoring mandates that broke with the traditions of culture. Early feminists paved the way for the equality that women enjoy today. But we struggle to connect with many contemporary feminists, especially those who seem to be in a ceaseless state of agitation...

Today, when a woman calls herself a feminist, it is not always clear what she means. The definition of feminism itself has changed a lot since its inception...

Hopefully, as you come to understand feminism's history and the three waves of feminism, you will see not only the more redeeming aspects of ages past but learn how to advocate for a healthier feminism in times to come.

Mama Bear Apologetics, pages 236-237

ACTIVE READING NOTES

READING FOCUS:	MY RESPONSE:
Before you read:	
After skimming the chapter title and subheads, what is one question you would like to have answered in the chapter?	My question:
While you read:	
Vocabulary: Here you will list three words *you* found in the chapter and a few words we want to make sure you found.	My words: Book words: (You'll define these in the **Digging Deeper** section later in this lesson.)
After you read:	
Answer: Did you find an answer to your pre-reading question? (We hope so.) If yes, record it to the right.	My answer:
"Aha!" Moments: List three things you highlighted or underlined in the chapter. This can be new information you learned or encouraging reinforcements of things you knew. Or just plain anything that popped out at you.	My "Aha!" moments: 1. 2. 3.

EMPOWERING WORDS

- *Oppression*—A cruel or excessive exercise of power.

- *Misogyny*—Classically, a hatred or mistrust of women.

- *Sexism* (usually with regard to men against women)—To discriminate against or treat a person according to their gender stereotype and their individual characteristics (for example, all women love to cook).

- *Patriarchy* (classic definition)—A system in which the father is the head of the household (literally, "rule of fathers").

- *Patriarchy* (current definition)—Society in which men are the dominant rulers.

- *Monolithic*—Those who adhere to the same beliefs.

EMPOWERING THOUGHTS

Sometimes we feel caught between a rock and hard place with feminism. Though we appreciate the freedoms won by our foremother feminists (like writing a book under my own name!), we may not feel comfortable aligning with modern-day feminists. This is because the ideas of feminism have changed drastically, but the *title* of feminist has not. Whenever someone calls themselves a feminist (or calls you one!), ask: "What do you mean when you use the term *feminist?*"

Read Genesis 5:1-2. In verse 1, *how* does God make man?

How does He do it (hint: note the prepositional phrase)?

In verse 2, what three things does God do?

—

—

—

Who did God name "Man"?

What can we learn about God's perspective on gender from Genesis 5:1-2?

DIGGING DEEPER

1. To better understand how feminism has changed, it's helpful to know the distinctives that mark the different waves of feminism.

Explain the differences between first-, second-, and third-wave feminism (pages 237-241):

Wave of Feminism	View of Women	Stated Goals
First-wave egalitarian		
First-wave maternal		
Second wave		
Third wave		

2. What legitimate equalities did the first-wave feminists—both egalitarian and maternal—work together to forge (page 238)?

3. Read the Betty Friedan quote on pages 239-240. List four of the (many) very strong claims she makes:

——

——

—

—

a. Do you agree or disagree with these claims? Why?

b. On page 244, we see that the word *patriarchy* has been hijacked. Historically this word had a positive meaning. Now patriarchy is considered an evil. Why was order and authority within the family so necessary in Bible times?

c. How would you describe the difference between *protective* and *oppressive?*

It's time to Roar Like a Mother at feminism!

Recognize the Message

4. In your own words, what is modern-day feminism?

5. Which three of the four messages of feminism do you think are the most prevalent, and why (pages 241-242)?

—

—

—

Offer Discernment

6. Identify and explain one or more things that we can learn from feminism (that is, what truths does it offer, or what motives can we dignify?). List as many as you can think of, including those in the book.

7. In your own words, explain this statement on page 243: "A victim who is desperate to be heard will overlook the flaws of a movement that is willing to listen and be angry on their behalf." Have you seen this happen in other movements?

8. Identify and explain which five of the six lies smuggled in with feminism you think are the most prevalent, and why (pages 244-246).

—

—

—

—

—

Argue for a Healthier Approach

9. Choose one to three of the truths you identified above and interact with them. How does a balanced biblical approach achieve the goals or affirm the truths that the proponents of feminism are offering? Bonus points for scripture references!

10. "Hurting people hurt people." Explain how this fact can influence our attitude toward angry feminists.

Reinforce Through Discussion, Discipleship, and Prayer

11. Your son comes home crying because a girl at school told him that he was everything that was wrong with the world because he's a boy. You know that the girl in question is rumored to have an abusive father. How can you help your son understand the likely causes for the girl's anger, while helping him realize that he is not at fault for the sins of all men? How can understanding the causes for someone's anger help us to live at peace and understanding with them, despite disagreeing with their conclusions? How do you ROAR through your son's experience?

12. You and your children are walking through a retail store and you see a display of products that say "Girl Power" on them. Ask them if they have ever seen something with "Boy Power" on it. Most likely they haven't. Ask them: "Why don't we see that message?" This might help you get a better idea of what messages your children have already ingested from feminism.

KEY SCRIPTURES

We encourage you to read the following verses in context (read at least the entire chapter), reflect on how they relate to what you're learning, and thank God for the hope and guidance found in His Word.

- *Galatians 3:28*—"There is neither Jew nor Greek, there is neither slave nor free, there is no male and female, for you are all one in Christ Jesus."

- *Matthew 7:3*—"Why do you see the speck that is in your brother's eye, but do not notice the log that is in your own eye?"

- *Psalm 28:3*—"Do not drag me off with the wicked, with the workers of evil, who speak peace with their neighbors while evil is in their hearts."

- *Proverbs 4:14*—"Do not enter the path of the wicked, and do not walk in the way of the evil."

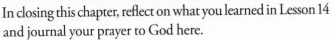

PAWS FOR PRAYER

In closing this chapter, reflect on what you learned in Lesson 14 and journal your prayer to God here.

Praise:

Admit:

Worship with thanksgiving:

Supplication (ask):

CHRISTIANITY NEEDS A MAKEOVER—*PROGRESSIVE CHRISTIANITY*

Now imagine that all the "isms" you've read about so far in this book are options in a soda dispenser. Grab a cup labeled "Christian," go down the line and put in a little bit of everything. A little bit of new spirituality, pluralism, self-helpism, feminism, Marxism, relativism, naturalism, skepticism, postmodernism, and emotionalism. What new libation will you have created? You will be quenching your spiritual thirst with an effervescent fusion of ideas called—progressive Christianity. But be warned: *This* mixture isn't harmless like the one I made at the pizza joint. These ideas have life-and-death consequences.

Mama Bear Apologetics, pages 253-254

ACTIVE READING NOTES

READING FOCUS:	MY RESPONSE:
Before you read:	
After skimming the chapter title and subheads, what is one question you would like to have answered in the chapter?	My question:

While you read:	
Vocabulary: Here you will list three words *you* found in the chapter and a few words we want to make sure you found.	My words:
After you read:	
Answer: Did you find an answer to your pre-reading question? (We hope so.) If yes, record it to the right.	My answer:
"Aha!" Moments: List three things you high-lighted or underlined in the chapter. This can be new information you learned or encouraging reinforcements of things you knew. Or just plain anything that popped out at you.	My "Aha!" moments: 1. 2. 3.

EMPOWERING WORDS

- *German higher criticism*—Movement that denies the Bible's supernatural origins (such as the fact it is God-breathed) and seeks to explain its meaning strictly from the perspective of the humans who wrote it and the culture in which they wrote.

- *Early twentieth-century liberalism*—A trend in theological thinking that resulted from the premises of German higher criticism and that placed human reason above divine revelation (since, according to German higher criticism, there was no supernatural help in writing the Bible).

- *Theology*—The study of God and religious truths as described in Scripture.

- *Creed*—A concise statement that attempts to summarize the main doctrines of one's beliefs (for example, the apostles' creed).

- *Doctrine of Inspiration*—The teaching that God divinely influenced the human authors of the Scriptures in such a way that what they wrote was the very Word of God; it was God-breathed.

- *Hyperfundamentalism*—A radical and unbiblical form of Christianity often characterized by extreme loyalty to movements or leaders, militant stances on nonessentials, inability to receive correction, anti-intellectual bias, strong political involvement, and double standards for personal ethics/hypocrisy.

- *Exclusivity of Christianity*—The biblical teaching that Jesus is the only way to God.

EMPOWERING THOUGHTS

Deconstruction stories seem to be hitting social media feeds with increasing frequency these days. On page 255 we read that this journey starts by questioning some historic Christian beliefs.

In the left column below, list the seven historic Christian beliefs in question (see top of page 255). In the right column, explain these beliefs in your own words.

Historic Christian Belief	My Explanation
1.	
2.	

3.	
4.	
5.	
6.	
7.	

DIGGING DEEPER

1. After dismantling the historic Christian beliefs, what new beliefs or official creeds does progressive Christianity uphold (page 256)?

2. What is the "sin" that sets progressive Christians running?

3. Living without set rules (or essential doctrines) can sound wonderful on the surface. Yet when we do so, we lose far more than we might gain. Explain, in your own words, what is lost when we abandon official creeds or belief statements with regard to our faith,

such as the historical fact of the resurrection, the reality of sin, the inerrancy of Scripture, etc.

4. On page 258, we read that progressive leader Brian McLaren suggests Christians should change the way they read the Bible.

   a. What new approach does he recommend?

   b. To what does he compare Scripture?

5. Think carefully about the consequences of lowering the role and trustworthiness of Scripture as progressive Christians do. Give one example of how you, as a Christ-follower, would be affected if the Bible is—as progressive Christianity asserts—merely a human collection of diary entries written by our unenlightened ancestors.

It's time to Roar Like a Mother at progressive Christianity!

Recognize the Message

6. In your own words, what is progressive Christianity?

7. Which four of the five messages of progressive Christianity do you think are the most prevalent/concerning, and why (pages 257-260)?

—

—

—

—

Offer Discernment

8. What are some of the legitimate critiques that progressive Christianity has brought to light (page 260)?

9. Using these legitimate critiques, progressive Christians have

arrived at some wrong conclusions. Give one example of this (page 260).

Argue for a Healthier Approach

10. How can we avoid extremes and develop a healthy and biblical faith (page 261)?

11. What are the two extremes that constantly react to each other within progressive Christianity?

12. How can we embrace the truths offered up by progressive Christians without embracing an opposite extreme (pages 261-262)?

13. The Old Testament is referenced nearly 300 times in the New Testament, with some 30 of those references from Jesus himself. Here are a few examples: Matthew 22:29; 26:54-56; Mark 14:49.

    a. What can we learn about Jesus's view of the Scriptures from these verses?

b. With that in mind, read Luke 24:44. What did Jesus say about the Old Testament Scriptures?

c. Considering Jesus's extensive use of the Old Testament in His teaching, how might we respond to people who believe the God of the Old Testament is a moral monster, whereas Jesus, from the New Testament, is said to be a wonderful, peaceful teacher and social justice activist? Would Jesus—the one whom they claim is superior to the God of the Old Testament—agree? Why or why not?

14. What is the key difference between progressive Christianity and historic Christianity (page 262)?

Reinforce Through Discussion, Discipleship, and Prayer

15. Many who deconstruct to progressive Christianity (or even atheism) state the following common contributing experiences: being raised in legalistic churches, experiencing spiritual abuses of power, dealing with hypocritical Christians, and having no safe place

to express doubts. How can these commonalities in deconstruction stories help us to choose a church home for our families?

16. As parents, we want our children to have a solid, unwavering faith. Sometimes their doubts and questions can cause us to jump to the worst-case scenario: *My child is unsaved!* But the Bible is filled with examples of spiritual heroes who dealt with doubt. Even John the Baptist (who heard the audible voice of God the Father clearly identifying Jesus's true identity) doubted who Jesus was when life got tough (Matthew 11:2-3).

a. With deconstruction stories on one hand and a balanced biblical view of doubt on the other, describe how you hope to respond to your children's spiritual doubts in the future.

b. Read Hebrews 11:1. How can our children's doubts (and our own) become building blocks for a more robust faith?

KEY SCRIPTURES

We encourage you to read the following verses in context (read at least the entire chapter), reflect on how they relate to what you're learning, and thank God for the hope and guidance found in His Word.

- *John 16:33*—"I have said these things to you, that in me you may have peace. In the world you will have tribulation. But take heart; I have overcome the world."

- *1 John 1:8*—"If we say we have no sin, we deceive ourselves, and the truth is not in us."

- *2 Timothy 4:3*—"The time is coming when people will not endure sound teaching, but having itching ears they will accumulate for themselves teachers to suit their own passions."

- *Galatians 1:9*—"As we have said before, so now I say again: If anyone is preaching to you a gospel contrary to the one you received, let him be accursed." (See 1 Corinthians 15 for a great summary of the original gospel.)

PAWS FOR PRAYER

In closing this chapter, reflect on what you learned in Lesson 15 and journal your prayer to God here.

Praise:

Admit:

Worship with thanksgiving:

Supplication (ask):

ANSWERS TO QUIZ
ON PAGES 61-62

1. Premodern

2. Modern

3. Postmodern

4. Premodern

5. Modern

6. Premodern

7. Postmodern

8. Postmodern

9. Postmodern

10. Premodern

ANSWERS TO QUIZ
ON PAGE 76

- *The Bible was reliably transmitted*—This can be tested based on evidence by studying the various manuscripts and the dates they were transmitted and comparing them against each other.

- *Believers are going to heaven*—This is a faith statement. We trust this is true because the Bible says it. But a key element to this faith is knowing that the Bible has been reliably transmitted (which is an evidential claim). Can you see how evidential statements and faith statements work together?

- *Jesus was a real person who lived, died, and rose again*—This is an evidential statement that can be supported with historical documents. People outside of Christianity wrote about Jesus.

- *Jesus's death means that we have eternal life*—This is a faith statement. But notice it is a faith statement that rests on the evidential claim that Jesus was a real person and the events of His life were reliably transmitted.

- *Sex outside of marriage is wrong*—This is a faith statement and an evidential statement. While it is a faith statement to say that sex outside of marriage is morally wrong, there is evidence that there are negative—and at times even devastating—consequences to bringing sex into nonmarital relationships.

- *The only true knowledge is that which can be tested with the scientific method*—This is a faith statement. Can we prove the truthfulness of this statement using the scientific method? No.

- *God is good*—This is a faith statement that can be supported by evidence based on the reliable transmission of factual events through which God showed his greatness. This claim can also be supported (though not proven) by personal experiences with God's goodness.

ANSWERS TO QUIZ
ON PAGES 86-87

a. God exists—objective statement; depends on the objective existence of God

b. Math is boring—subjective statement; some people love math

c. Stealing is wrong—objective statement; this is true for all people

d. My brother is annoying—subjective statement; some people like a person for the same qualities that you think are annoying

e. There is no such thing as absolute truth—objective statement (and a self-refuting one!)

f. My teacher hates me—probably a subjective statement! (But I don't know your kid...)